A NECESSARY END

D1494893

8/12

Hertfordshire
COUNTY COUNCIL
Community Information

22 AUG 2003

1 2 NOV 2003

SUFFOLK
19/2/09.

202.
3
NEC

2 1 DEC 2002   2 0 NOV 2009

27 FEB 2003

16 MAY 2003

Please renew/return this item by the last date shown.

So that your telephone call is charged at local rate,
please call the numbers as set out below:

	From Area codes 01923 or 020:	From the rest of Herts:
Renewals:	01923 471373	01438 737373
Enquiries:	01923 471333	01438 737333
Minicom:	01923 471599	01438 737599

L32   www.hertsdirect.org

A NECESSARY END

Attitudes to Death

edited by Julia Neuberger and
John A. White

PAPERMAC

First published 1991 by
PAPERMAC
a division of Macmillan Publishers Limited
Cavaye Place London SW10 9PG
and Basingstoke

Associated companies in Auckland, Delhi, Dublin, Gaborone,
Hamburg, Harare, Hong Kong, Johannesburg, Kuala Lumpur,
Lagos, Manzini, Melbourne, Mexico City, Nairobi, New York,
Singapore and Tokyo

ISBN 0–333–48276–X

A CIP catalogue record for this book is available from
the British Library

Typeset by Macmillan Production Limited
Printed in Hong Kong

Seeing that death, a necessary end,
Will come when it will come.
Julius Caesar, II. ii. 29–30

CONTENTS

ACKNOWLEDGEMENTS

The publishers thank the following for their kind permission to reproduce copyright material: Faber and Faber Ltd for the extracts from *Murder in the Cathedral* by T. S. Eliot, *Four Quartets* by T. S. Eliot and *The Whitsun Weddings* by Philip Larkin; Pattern Music Ltd for the extract from 'Graceland' by Paul Simon; David Higham Associates for the extract from 'Do not go gentle into that good night' by Dylan Thomas; Editions du Seuil for the extract from Teilhard de Chardin's *Le Milieu divin*, © Editions du Seuil, 1957. Every effort has been made to trace all copyright holders, but if any have been inadvertently overlooked, we apologise. Redress will be made in future editions.

ACKNOWLEDGEMENTS

INTRODUCTION

Rabbi Julia Neuberger

Julia Neuberger lives in London and West Cork, Ireland. She trained at Leo Baeck College, London, where she now lectures part-time, and she served the South London Liberal Synagogue for twelve years. She is a visiting fellow at the King's Fund Institute, London, working on research ethics committees in the NHS, chairs the Patients Association, is a council member of the North London Hospice Group and a trustee of the Runnymede Trust and the Citizenship Foundation. She is also a Council Member of St George's House, Windsor, and involved in interfaith dialogue. She is a frequent broadcaster and contributes regularly to a variety of newspapers and magazines.

A gradual change has come about in Britain in attitudes to death and dying. What was once unmentionable is now the stuff of common parlance, particularly when the discussion is about hospices, or those extra-angelic nurses in the Macmillan team. Many books have been published recounting people's own experiences in the face of their oncoming deaths, though none, thus far, as moving as Peter Noll's account (*In the Face of Death*, Viking, 1990) of what it feels like to have refused treatment by choice. There have been personal accounts of encounters with death, including Rosemary Dinnage's selection of interviews in her *Ruffian on the Stair* (Viking, 1990). There have been books for professionals trying to come to terms

1

with the psychology of grief, including the grief of 'those who are leaving this world', rather than the hitherto commonplace studies of the grief of those who are left within it. And there have been television programmes and even a *Which?* publication, telling people what to do when a death occurs.

But none of these begins to explore how people of different cultures, backgrounds and faiths look at death, personally but dispassionately, as their own moment of death approaches. None attempts to explore those extraordinary variations, partly the product of our human personalities in all their strange guises, partly the result of our differing upbringings with their cultural and religious variations, that make us look at ourselves and our inevitable mortality in such different ways.

In this volume, we have asked people of very different views and backgrounds to speak for themselves, having been encouraged by their editors to look at particular questions. They were asked what they felt about the concepts of immortality, of life after death. They were asked to set death in a context which they felt was reasonable, approachable for themselves, and possible for their readers to understand. They were asked to struggle with new perceptions of what death actually means, in the wake of scientific discoveries which have cast inevitable doubt upon such concepts as the soul and the life hereafter.

Our contributors have approached this task in widely varying ways. Some, unsurprisingly, have felt constrained to stick fairly closely to a form of religious orthodoxy. As editors, we dare not question whether that, in their heart of hearts, is what they really feel. Others are distinctly heterodox in their views, throwing a cool glance at the classical theologians before treading new paths, and relying upon imagination and intellect

2

combined, rather than on the traditional approach, in order to produce a more personal account. And some have tried to do that hardest of tasks: to combine the two.

That is particularly the case with those who represent religions less familiar to western readers, such as Islam, Buddhism or Sikhism. They feel an implied duty to explain as well as to reflect, and have attempted to do just that. But they have also discussed their personal views, making a contribution all the more valuable when those personal reflections are ones with which so few Jews or Christians are familiar.

Then there are curious comparisons to be drawn, between such similarities of approach as those of Rabbi Jonathan Magonet and Dr Zaki Badawi, Jew and Muslim, whose rootedness in religions of the Book and of the law is dramatically apparent as they both steer away from some of their own orthodoxies. There are the fascinating differences of emphasis between our Anglican contributors – the orthodoxy, to some extent at least, of the Bishop of Oxford, the Rt Reverend Richard Harries, on the one hand, and a more questioning contribution from General Sir Hugh Beach on the other.

We should not be surprised at all this variation. Though half the contributors are, broadly speaking, Christian, they share very little except their labels. They range from the theologian to the soldier, from the academic mind to the practical mind, and they give their personal impressions and thoughts rather than a party line. What is fascinating is the contrasts within Christianity as represented here, as well as the contrasts between Christian contributors and the others.

All through our initial contemplation of this project ran a sense that somehow the established orthodoxies were barely held amongst many thinking people who question, sometimes reject, established belief in the afterlife, in immortality, in the soul. All too often we hear people of apparently pronounced religious faith admit that they believe that death is simply the final goodnight and goodbye. There is no more physical or spiritual. Beyond death, only nothingness waits for us, and all the theology, all the doctrine, are there only to give us comfort.

One argument for all the doctrine about life everlasting, or a world to come, is that it creates a moral imperative for human beings. To reach that desired state of being allowed into the next world, or being resurrected, good behaviour and total obedience to the codes of law and teaching are essential. How else are human beings to be convinced that they need to keep in line, and what other hold do priests and teachers have over their flocks, if they can not promise Hell everlasting, or at least the absence of true joy in Heaven?

Nor can we entirely discount wishful thinking. For those who cannot bear to contemplate their own mortality, the expression of desire for an afterlife, whether in the liturgy or in theological tracts, is almost as good as the belief in its existence. If we so use the optative mood to express our longing for a world to come, then, by its insertion into the liturgy, the texts of religious faith, the common parlance, it will come to be, even though the basis for it in the earliest texts of revelation is hard to find. The doctrine of physical resurrection of the dead, for instance, only appears to have entered Judaism as a result of its losing ground to the new religion of Christianity. There is no resurrection, physical or otherwise, in the Hebrew Bible, other than the Witch of Endor summoning up Samuel the Prophet from the dead (I Samuel 28:7), arguably not resurrection as commonly understood, and the vision of the valley of the dry bones in Ezekiel (Ezekiel 37:1–14), a vision of national rebirth

4

rather than of individual physical resurrection. The afterlife itself is ill-defined, if it exists at all. There is Sheol, in all probability a shady pit. Its definition is that of colourlessness. It is to be feared because it marks the end of life, but it is no hell with torment and punishment; it is, rather, a place of nothingness, somewhere below earth level. It was of little significance in the Hebrew Bible, and its insignificance has continued into modern Judaism. More important has been the story of Elijah going up to heaven in a fiery chàriot, and not dying, not descending into Sheol. For within the Jewish tradition Elijah becomes the herald of the coming of the Messiah.

The Messianic age includes the ingathering of the exiles, and at that stage there will also be the physical resurrection of humanity which is usually linked to the Day of Judgment or the End of Days. Until that point, Sheol is insignificant; we are told little about it, and the clear emphasis in the Hebrew Bible is on this life, this world, these people, the here and now.

Yet, in the second century or thereabouts, the rabbis felt sufficiently disquieted by the growth of Christianity (and perhaps some of the mystery cults of Asia Minor) to drag in the concept of physical resurrection, having already begun to introduce spiritual immortality and the concept of a world to come somewhat earlier.

But it was not necessarily merely to provide comfort for those who had an apparently unfair deal in this life, or for those who could not bear the idea of an imminent and total end, that the concept of immortality and res-urrection entered Judaism, or indeed any other religion. Such a view of the world, that there is another life to come, that we will answer for our misdeeds in this world when we reach the next, is also profoundly disturbing. For it switches the emphasis on the place of human endeavour and its purpose away from the present, and it allows the notion of suffering in this world gaining its reward in a world to come.

Therefore notions of the afterlife can do something quite other than provide comfort. They can induce terror. For people fear what they are likely to encounter in that world to come where final judgment will be given. They know that they have not done all they should in this world, nor been everything to their families and friends that they ought to have been. With what terror then must they go into death, heart in mouth, believing that they are about to undergo a form of punishment which the human mind cannot even contemplate.

And what control that must have given, has given, the religious leaders who told these stories, encouraged this view amongst their flocks. They could persuade, cajole, and ultimately terrify people into doing whatever they wanted, in the name of church or synagogue or mosque, on the basis that only by compliance would they avoid that terrible fate awaiting them after their deaths. Nor is that wholly a thing of the past.

It is extraordinary, historically, that though there was huge emphasis upon human fate after death, particularly within Christianity, the other strong tradition, before death became an unmentionable subject altogether, was to die 'the good death'. Obviously the two traditions are linked. It was not possible to die the good death if one was gibbering and terrified whilst consciousness remained; rather, it was a virtue to die quietly, peacefully, prayerfully, with family around one. The search for the good death during the seventeenth and eighteenth centuries led to considerable discussion of its merits.

It is that tradition which the hospice movement has, in some sense, adopted. Crucial to its philosophy is the desire to alleviate pain. 'Pain-control' is the watchword, because in pain human beings find it hard to experience the good death; they merely suffer and can gain nothing from those around them, nor give anything to them. Obviously there are religious traditions where a wholly different view prevails. Buddhism, with its emphasis on rebirth, sees death merely as part of the cycle, though from a Buddhist perspective, death is the most important 'life crisis', since it stands at the point of transition from one life to another. The ideal is to die in a conscious state which is also calm and uplifted. Thus it would be preferable not to die drugged and unconscious. Indeed, there are Buddhist traditions in which the use of pain relief is seen as detrimental, in that it reduces awareness. The ultimate goal of the Buddhist is to go into that next life fully aware, indeed, at the most heightened state of awareness imaginable.

It also has to be said that many of the techniques used by Buddhists in their approach to their end are pain-relieving techniques of the Buddhist meditation schools. They do not involve the use of drugs, the palliation therapy so perfected by the hospice movement, but use instead the concentration of the mind in meditation to override pain and to face the end with equanimity.

This equanimity is reached at the highest stage of awareness, the state required in order to make the journey to the next world, the next existence. There is, all through this collection of essays, a fundamental divide between those who believe there is a next world to go to, and those who feel that this is it. Jonathan Magonet, for instance, in his discussion of Jewish attitudes, makes the excellent point that Judaism is always loosely described as the religion of 'this-worldly' concerns, in contrast with the 'other-worldly' concerns of Christianity, and that this is far too simplistic. Both are big enough for this-worldly and next-worldly concerns but Judaism is, on the whole,

7

more comforting about the next world. The rabbis argued that only four biblical characters were such great sinners that they did not have a share in the world to come, and there is even some debate within the texts to suggest that the rabbis wished even further to reduce the number who would not inherit the delights of the world to come. To what extent this was a serious debate and to what extent it merely demonstrates the unwillingness of the rabbis to consign even the worst of sinners to having no future is unclear. The point remains, however, that the tradition gives everyone a share in that world after death, and does not glory in the idea of eternal punishment, or nothingness, for anyone.

Jonathan Magonet does not quite believe that the afterlife as expressed by the rabbis is what he, or progressive Judaism, believes in. His emphasis lies elsewhere; he rehearses the attitudes to 'this-worldly' human suffering in considerable detail. This is where some of the contrasts lie. For Judaism, though it has a relatively unsophisticated doctrine of reward in the next life after sufferings in this world, nevertheless argues much more consistently for a self-examination if sufferings are heavy, to see if they have been brought about by one's own actions, and, much more profoundly and, to my mind, relevantly, whether they are what rabbinic literature describes as the chastisements of love, which are to improve the individual in some way, or the tests imposed by the divine to see if the individual can withstand or cope with grief and pain.

In some ways, this produces a very cruel picture of God but it needs to be viewed in the context of a total relationship with a divine being, with pleasures and pain being meted out in equal measure as a test of how the human frame and personality will cope. At one level, this is a primitive, overly personal approach but the view that sets all of life's experiences in the form of an examination paper, to see how well one can deal with whatever fate sends, or, more likely, whatever is the knock-on effect of what one has already done oneself, is not unfamiliar to me. A hero is not someone who necessarily shows inordinate bravery on the battlefield but may be the person who deals with dignity, courage and forbearance with all the crises life presents. Such people have been tested and not found wanting.

But if life is about being tested, about a challenge to see how one can respond to it here and now, then what does death have to say to us, other than that we should strive to be in good emotional and spiritual shape to meet it?

The old picture of life beginning at the moment of conception, with a cell growing into a baby and a person without interruption or deviation, is beginning to look suspect in the wake of scientific discoveries about the development of the embryo, about the life-force of the sperm or the ovum, about our capacity to create human life in a test-tube when it could not be created in the conventional way within the mother's womb. Those developments throw into disarray our concepts of life and death. Our picture of world order is challenged by concepts of chaos, and our conviction that everything has a purpose may or may not be supported by the new theoretical physics, which is beginning to suggest an element, if not of purpose, at least of design in the universe, rather than of random chance. To view human death without seeing it in the context of the whole of human development is both to over-individualise it and, in some odd way, to trivialise the rest of creation.

There is a question, to which the answer is supposed to be so blindingly obvious that it brings us comfort, which is often asked to help us see human lives in perspective:

which would we prefer – life for ever, as it is, for each of us, without change, no new births, no children, no young love, no excitement; or death as we have it, but with birth alongside it, laughing children, new life and new hopes? That is not a reasonable choice to be asked to make, and the question begins to look more than a little absurd when we examine the continuum of human existence which rules out such a choice. It is a romantic illusion to say that there can be no doubt that we would prefer to have death as it is, and young life alongside. Although true in the general picture of things, for those of us who have a remarkably well-developed fear of death, eternal life in this world might well seem preferable.

It is in this area that I feel most in need of developing my own thoughts for, in so far as it is possible, I want to go beyond the intensely individual experience to look at life and patterning in the universe. If it is the case that theoretical physicists are beginning to demonstrate that there is a design in the universe, then perhaps we could look at that design and see ourselves as tiny creatures within that pattern, that ordered universe. If we can succeed in seeing ourselves in that way, perhaps it will lead us into beginning to extrapolate from that designed universe a sense of human purpose, as part of that greater whole.

Taking that sense of human purpose, we then have to ask ourselves where that purpose lies, in this world or the next, or, indeed, in a combination of the two. Speaking entirely personally, though unable, of course, to reject the Jewish tradition from which I come, that purpose must lie in this world. That is not to deny completely a world to come (though I have such hazy hints of its existence that for this purpose I might as well say that it is not there in any way that matters), but it is to say that the field of endeavour, the scene of human purpose,

10

seems to be the here and now. I have a great fear of
the damage we can inflict upon ourselves by trying to
live our lives as if there were another world to come,
and find the assertion by Rabbi Tarfon in *The Ethics of
the Fathers* (Mishnah Pirkei, Avoth 2:16) that 'The day
is short and the task is great and the labourers are idle
and the wage is abundant and the master of the house
is pressing,' more important than any statement about
who has a share in the next world.

The task is great in *this* world. The Master is pressing
us to get things right in *this* world. Once we recognise a
pattern in human existence, we can start also to recognise
the role of human endeavour, that of 'tikkun olam', the
establishing of the right order of things here in this world.
Born innocent, we learn from the example of our elders
and from our experience of temptation that it is easy to
sin. We start off as tiny specks too small to see without
a microscope, and we develop into beings who can make
choices, who, the older we get, can make increasingly
reasoned and sometimes reasonable choices. As adults,
we have the capacity to make fully informed choices, if
we make the effort, and it is in our hands to do both right
and wrong, to improve or to make worse the affairs of our
homes, offices, cities and societies.

This is the adult picture of life. For children, for babies,
it is different. Their choices cannot be made. They are not
yet fully part of the continuum of existence. Judaism does
not even give a full funeral to a baby who dies before it is
thirty days old (although that child acquires personhood,
taking precedence over its mother's life, when it is beginning to emerge from the womb). Though I have problems
with that view for pastoral reasons, since I regard
funerals as being largely for the survivors, and since
parents need to mark that loss most profoundly, it does
suggest an idea of human continuum. Our life grows and

flourishes. Our death is at a moment, but just as life is a continuum as it begins, so too death is often not of the moment alone, but of a process, another continuum.

There are those who die instantly in fatal accidents or from massive heart-attacks of which they know nothing, but most of us are not like that. We have time to contemplate our own deaths, our own dying, and we give our loved ones time to come to terms with it as well. We die slowly, sometimes too slowly, with medical intervention which we would prefer not to have for ourselves and not to see for others whose eyes tell us that this is not what they had desired at their end. We are subjected to surgery, chemotherapy, to treatments which we find degrading. Yet we are assured we will have life of some quality at the end.

In Judaism, this-life affirming as it is, we have a major problem coming to terms with the idea that sometimes it might be kinder not to treat. Perhaps, once on that continuum of dying, which all of us are from the moment of our birth, we need to decide at what point our lives in this world are worth fighting for, and to what extent. We need to begin to see ourselves as able to make choices about our deaths and dying. That is not to say that we can ask for euthanasia, for that puts an intolerable burden of decision-making upon those whose duty it is to care for us, not to kill us. We do not have the right to ask them to take on that responsibility. But we can ask for more and more pain relief, blotting out awareness as Buddhists would see it. We can also ask not to be treated, or to interrupt the treatment, because the treatment seems worse than the disease, and knowingly curtail our living time by months or even years. We can say, at some point which only we can decide, 'Enough! I want no more. I have tried to fight; I have suffered what I am prepared to suffer. Let me go into that good night.'

On the whole, my Jewish tradition feels strongly opposed to such a view. Life is to be preserved at all costs. People are not even to be told they are dying, at the most extreme end of the spectrum, lest they stop fighting and therefore shorten their lives by a few hours or days. Yet unless we begin to see death not as a moment but as a process, not always out of our control but sometimes so dramatically within it that doctors and nurses look on amazed as we go contrary to all the apparent laws of nature and science, we fail to learn the lesson that life sets us. How often do grandmothers stay alive deliberately to see their great-grandchild born? They hold the baby in their arms and die the next day, content. Fathers stay alive, massive coronaries notwithstanding, to marry off their daughters before they too die content, their short-term mission fulfilled. It is too common a phenomenon to ignore, and it tells us all we need to know about the human psyche being able to override physical weakness and medical expectations. We live, as we die, on a continuum. We do what we can in this world. We make our choices and try to hold on to a code of good conduct. We never do enough. But in the end, death is not fearful. It can even be welcome, a release from pain of body or mind or soul. It can release agony, and give us the sense, however hard we find it to justify rationally, that we are going to be near our dear ones in some kind of hereafter, even if that place is merely the immortality we achieve in the minds of those we leave behind.

For me, this is the lesson of death. It is nothing to fear of itself, but it concentrates the mind powerfully in examining what it is we mean by life. Not only does it challenge what we mean by birth, but it also challenges everything we say when we talk about development, adulthood, old age. If all of this is merely a continuum, if we are born on a road to death, then it is a sense of the value of that intervening gap that we have to acquire. For if we only get one go, as I believe we do, I want to be able to look in the mirror and see, not Cary Grant as Stewart Sutherland so wittily imagines, or even Snow White, but myself, old if possible, worn and used as a human frame can be, but at least partially satisfied, feeling that it was worthwhile.

This is a very personal view, with all the markings of the religious and social group from which I come. I make no apology for that, for the exploration of these issues can only be a very personal one, once the theology has been examined, held in the palm and turned around, over and over, bits accepted and others rejected. Each author in this collection has tried to do that. They reveal much about themselves in the process and, taken together, present a picture of how thinking men and women of different faiths, cultures and backgrounds in Britain today look at these questions and find their own answers, incomplete, halting, and difficult though they may be.

SISTER DEATH

General Sir Hugh Beach

After Winchester and Cambridge, Hugh Beach spent forty years as a regular soldier with the Royal Engineers, which period included a spell in battle during the Second World War. Following in the footsteps of Marlborough and Wellington, he became Master General of the Ordinance, which included for him a seat on the Army Board. Throughout these years he has also been a member of the Third Order of the Anglican Society of St Francis, which seeks under the direction of the Friars to put the Franciscan ideals into practice in ordinary daily life. He was for three years Director of the Council for Arms Control and has a special interest in the application of Christian Ethics to the art of war. He has three sons and a daughter and reckons skiing and sailing to be his chief recreations.

My mother was much hemmed in by deaths. She loved her two brothers and they both died young. The elder, a far-seeing sapper officer, became a pioneer of army flying and was killed in an air crash at Hendon, piloting his Bleriot, in 1910. The younger, a dashing gunner, was highly decorated in the First World War but badly blown up. Weakened by this he died of a lung infection at Hyderabad a few years later. Though as a child I had known this uncle quite well, and liked him very much, my mother could never bring herself to tell me he had died. Worse still, her first offspring, a baby

15

girl, died in Simla when only a few months old. My
father was by now in his mid-fifties, having married late
and then gone off to the war in Mesopotamia for nearly
five years. My parents tried once more and got me. No
chances were taken. I was born in London and bedded
out in Surrey with a grandmother until my parents
finally came back from India. Coddled by nannies and
governesses till the age of eight, I was sent to boarding
school at Broadstairs, where the air was said to be good
and the doctors competent. One holiday I had a tummy
pain and my mother distinctly heard the voice of her
younger brother saying, 'Get a doctor, Maud.' She did so
and the diagnosis was an enlarged appendix on the point
of rupture. It was removed by a doyen of the Royal College
of Surgeons in an expensive London nursing home. Next
year, despite the good air, I caught pneumonia at school.
This was before the days of penicillin. A small dormitory
was cleared for me, nurses hired, the school hushed for
the few vital days while expert nursing had its effect and
my life was saved.

On arrival at Winchester the house doctor, examining
me for freedom from skin infection of the groin, com-
mented that I had a very poor physique. After this I took
it for granted that I was weak and weedy, shortcomings
offset only by an efficient brainbox. It was a surprise and
relief when I was accepted by the army doctors five years
later (it being now 1941) for training as an officer in the
Sappers. My twenty-first birthday party, such as it was,
took place at a country club in Essex, very late during
the preparations for the invasion of Normandy in June
1944.

By July I was in command of a small sapper party,
supporting a battalion of the Queen's Regiment in a night
attack, south of the village of La Vallée. Our task was
to clear the mines from a mile of gravel road through

the woods, so that personnel carriers and anti-tank guns could follow the infantry on to the objective, before the enemy counter-attacked at dawn. We did the job in time, but the first vehicle to go forward blew up on a mine which we had missed. The rest of the column stopped. I could not bear the thought that the infantry, unsupported, would have to fall back and that it would be all our fault. I sat on the front mudguard of the leading vehicle where, if there were another mine, I would be certain to be killed, and ordered it to move forward. The drivers accepted this gesture of confidence and the advance resumed.

In early September I was an engineer reconnaissance officer with a column of armoured cars (11th Hussars) in the van of a rapid and almost unopposed advance across northern France and Belgium. We came to the canal at La Bassée and a bridge was found. It was partly damaged, and the question was whether it was strong enough to carry the armoured cars and in due course guns and tanks. My task was to inspect it and report. There were snipers around and I approached with circumspection, on hands and knees, behind a low railway embankment. Seeing a small enemy party on the far bank, instead of continuing my covert reconnaissance as duty and prudence required, I could not resist opening fire. My weapon being a Sten gun, it was not surprising that I missed and the gun jammed. The Germans, stung into activity by the noise, replied in kind. One bullet, passing low over the rails, went on to skim my spine, removing one of the small bony protuberances and paralysing me from the waist down. I was rescued by my lance sergeant and taken to the nearest hospital, a convent in Arras. The nuns packed the wound and I was returned to the hands of the army medical services. After a time the numbness passed to be replaced by pain and hyper-sensitivity; later a lumbar puncture showed that there was no damage to the spinal cord. If the bullet had entered half an inch lower paralysis would have been permanent. The surgeon warned that I could expect severe arthritis of the spine in later life, but I took up rowing at Cambridge to flex the backbone, and this seems to have worked. At sixty-five I can still touch my toes, and do so ten times every morning.

Having proved to be a relatively successful soldier, and under intense pressure of family expectation, I set aside my own strong preferences for a career in medicine or the church and signed up for a lifelong engagement in the army. Medicine I have pursued by proxy through marrying a GP. I have never for a moment regretted either decision.

During the 1950s I had two further brushes with death while training in north–west Germany. The first occasion was when I was running a course on mine warfare for officers of the armoured corps. To demonstrate the effects of an anti-tank mine I arranged to detonate an equivalent amount of high explosive under the track of a disused tank hulk. The rules for such demonstrations say that when using high explosive for cutting steel the safety distance for spectators is 1000 yards. This seemed to me to destroy all realism and I stationed the spectators (with myself) in a deep road cutting only about 200 yards from the explosion. The bang and resulting cloud of ascending debris were highly satisfactory. Not long afterwards there came a noise like a ram-jet engine. It was caused by a complete track link descending almost vertically, a lethal projectile. It fell amongst us and buried itself harmlessly in the tarmac. Only by extraordinary good luck was no one killed.

The second occasion came at the end of a large exercise when, as squadron commander, I was leading my convoy back from the training area to barracks. Many would have left this to their second-in-command, pleading more urgent business back in camp. It was night and all were tired. I thought it better leadership to do the job myself. In that area there was a number of railway level-crossings ungated and unmanned. The rule was that convoys must station a motor-cycle despatch rider at each crossing to act as a traffic policeman: if a train were seen approaching he would stop the column. We approached one such crossing at a moment when all our motor-cyclists were already busy policing other tricky points. The correct action would have been to stop and wait until one caught up with us. Instead I said to my driver, 'We'll take a chance on this one,' and kept going. As we crossed the railway I saw the headlights of a train approaching at full speed less than a hundred yards away. It took a few moments to disentangle the radio headphones, scramble out of the Land-rover, and run back towards the crossing to stop others from following. Too late; the next vehicle came on across the rails and as it did so the train hit its trailer, scattering the contents violently and slewing the vehicle off the road. The train stopped and so did everything else. Once again, providentially, no one was hurt. In the ensuing board of enquiry I had only to account for a bent trailer, damaged cooking gear, and a cracked buffer belonging to the Deutsche Bundesbahn. It did not affect my future.

After these excitements my career quietly prospered. Our marriage produced four healthy children who duly grew up. Over a period of twenty years I rose in rank from major to major general with the prospect of more advancement to come. Brushes with death ceased. To entertain the family I took up skiing, which is full of hazards, but though one of the boys once nearly killed himself I never suffered more than a torn muscle. Later we took to sailing and that was a different matter. Gerald

Priestland once voiced his suspicion that the sea is a sort of blind spot in God's vision; His writ does not entirely run there. In Genesis 1:2, 'Darkness was upon the face of the deep. And the spirit of God moved upon the face of the waters . . .' It is as if the sea were there already, waiting for Him. As it waited for me.

By the mid-1970s I had progressed to the ownership of a 34-foot catamaran and cruised in her from South Brittany to the Outer Hebrides. Two of my sons raced her successfully to the Azores and back. One of these sons, together with myself and two friends, sailed her in the Round the Island race of 1978. When we got close to Ventnor, in a lumpy sea with no tide running and a headwind of around force five, the boat was suddenly hit by a freak combination of downdraught and sea which put her on her side. Catamarans are unstable in that position, and there was no time to do anything to right her. She rapidly inverted on top of us and we had to swim out from underneath. One gulp of inhaled water can be fatal; everything hinges on holding one's breath and not getting snagged. Luckily we were all in the cockpit, wearing neither safety harnesses nor personal buoyancy. I remembered to swim downwards to clear the safety lines, but actually emerged between two of them. As we bobbed up around the boat we all called out, and everyone was accounted for. The boat was perfectly at ease upside down; we climbed back on to her, wet but quite safe, the sea around us being thick with craft, and were soon rescued by a passing trimaran. Our boat was presently taken in tow, still upside down, by an RNVR vessel on exercise, but she sank off Spithead and was only salvaged inadvertently by a fisherman in his nets several months later. By that time the insurance owned her. I had had enough of multi-hulls and bought a conventional cruiser-racer later the same season.

This led, because she was that kind of boat, to

our entering the ocean-racing scene and in particular
the Fastnet race of 1979. This was the race during
which an unexpected storm blew up, 165 yachts retired,
twenty-three were sunk or abandoned, 136 crew members
saved by the rescue services and fifteen drowned. By good
fortune I had invited an old friend who was also a highly
experienced yachtsman (Marston Tickell) to join us for
this race. He told us what to do, and saved the boat. At
first, when the storm blew up at about midnight on 13/14
August, we lay ahull. This meant taking down all sail and
lying passively across the waves, letting the boat roll as
she would. Up to a point this was perfectly safe, but not
when a big wave coming at an angle thrust us violently
backwards through the water turning the boat through
180 degrees. When this had happened a second time we
changed tactics and ran off. This meant steering deliberately downwind, still with no sail set, making about
4 knots from the wind on the mast and hull, taking the
waves as far as possible on the stern. It can happen that
even without sails a boat is driven dangerously fast and
has to slow herself down by towing warps behind. This
helps to keep the stern pointing into the waves so long
as they come up parallel, but decreases its ability to
lift to them. Being some fifty miles into the Irish Sea
we had plenty of sea room, and saw no need to trail
warps, the boat behaving well. On several occasions
waves broke into the cockpit, filling it to the level
of the seats, but the main hatchway was watertight,
the crew well secured and the cockpit drains in time
took the water away. After about eighteen hours the
wind started to die down, so we turned and made our
way back by Land's End to Penzance. The crew were
undamaged apart from one split lip and I thought the
boat was also. But when she was lifted out at the end
of the season it was found that the rudder was cracked

and had almost broken away from the rudder post at its roots. This must have happened while lying ahull when we were hit by the big waves and swung around. If we had lost the rudder at that stage, and then gone on to lose our nerve and taken to the life raft, as some did, I doubt we would have survived.

In the subsequent ten years, though I have sailed with family and friends many hundreds of miles, and even won races, nothing has happened to match the dramas of 1978–9. The size of my boats has steadily diminished and with them the degree of venturesomeness with which I sail them. Now grandchildren are my favourite crew, and the boat is small enough to live at the bottom of the garden. The sea may get me yet, but it is more likely that the motorway will.

I move frequently between our home in darkest Hampshire and London via the M3. I used to suffer mildly from hay fever and one day my wife gave me an anti-histamine to reduce it. I also had a glass of beer for lunch, not realising the effects of that combination. On the way up to London in a Morris 1800 I awoke on the central reservation to find the grass going past on both sides at window level and about 40 miles an hour. Luckily there were no ditches, and the other traffic was so dumbfounded that they let me back into the fast lane, albeit travelling much more slowly, Since then I have fallen asleep at speed once more at least, hitting the kerb at an angle and then awaking, mercifully without bursting the tyre. Mid-afternoon at around 3 p.m. is a particularly susceptible time. It is dangerous and highly anti-social to doze off in this way, the more so that a few minutes' resting in a lay-by affords a complete remedy. The family know all this and are strangely philosophical about it, even when travelling as passengers. ('Grandfather always nods off when driving.') But there is no possible excuse.

If a cat has nine lives it seems that I have already expended ten. What is one to make of this? Having been baptised within three months of birth, confirmed in my teens and spent some fifteen years under a regime of daily Anglican worship, I am inclined to ponder this question from a Christian point of view, and several points come to mind. First, there seems to be something strange about the timing of these episodes: two potentially fatal illnesses around the age of ten; two brushes with death in battle at twenty-one; two near misses on training at thirty-three; two perilous moments at sea aged fifty-five; two close encounters on the motorway in my early sixties. If God, by the hand of Providence, plans my life why does he organise these incidents in pairs? John Polkinghorne, in his recent book *Science and Creation* (SPCK) has a fascinating chapter on the role of chance. 'It is inevitably a world', he says, 'of ragged edges, where order and disorder interlace each other and where the exploration of possibility by chance will lead not only to the evolution of systems of increasing complexity, endowed with new possibilities, but also to the evolution of systems imperfectly formed and malfunctioning.' Among the latter systems I have to include myself. Because, secondly, it is clear, I am sorry to say, that apart from childhood illnesses all the above instances have been caused mainly by my own bravado, impetuosity, the desire to cut a dash and failure to obey simple rules of prudence perfectly well known to me. In every instance I have put others beside myself at risk. Being naturally cautious and introverted I cannot explain why it is that I break out in these ways. Though we all have a dark and destructive side in our natures the idea of a death wish turned against myself is unconvincing. St Paul describes the problem in Romans 7:19 and 23: 'the evil which I would not, that I do ... I see another law in my members, warring against the law of my mind.' I am left feebly saying of these foolhardy actions that they seemed a good idea at the time! But thirdly, if I am to believe in an interventionist God, then it is plain that on these eight occasions at least he has stepped in to save me from my own foolishness. Why should he do this? I am tempted to feel a glow of gratitude that he is preserving me for some good work that only I can do. A Christian can hardly overdo his gratitude to God, but is not this version tinged with unwarrantable arrogance? Are there not better men enough without selecting me?

Which raises the disturbing thought that it might be the devil's work. The first work of theology that I read when I grew up was a war-time book by C. S. Lewis called *The Screwtape Letters*. These were short missives from senior demon Screwtape to a young fiend out on temptation duty working for the damnation of one particular soul. Screwtape ridicules the idea that the war is helpful to the devil's cause. Does the young fiend not realise that the man's death at this moment is exactly what the devil wants to avoid? As the full impact of the war draws nearer and the man's worldly hopes take a lower place in his mind – he is full of his defence work, forced to attend to his neighbours more than he has ever done before and liking it more than he expected, taken out of himself and daily increasing in conscious dependence on the Enemy (meaning of course on God) – the man 'will almost certainly be lost to us if he is killed to-night'.

Coming from a don, comparatively safe in war-time Oxford, perhaps this smacks a bit too much of what the ayatollahs tell their conscripts: that death in battle ensures a passage straight to heaven. Much as I enjoyed *Screwtape* at the time, I cannot recall that it did much to reassure me on this point as I made ready to go to war. My friends and I took it for granted, and said quite openly, that our chances of surviving individually could be no better than evens. I do not remember our being greatly distressed at this. We were excited at taking part, the ends more than justifying the prospective cost. No doubt we each privately expected to be among the survivors, and most of us were right.

But where Screwtape came much closer to the truth was in describing what would happen if only the man could be kept alive. The devil, he says, then has time itself for an ally. The long dull monotonous years of middle-aged prosperity are excellent campaigning weather. Prosperity knits a man to the world. He feels that he is finding his place in it while really it is finding its place in him. His increasing reputation, his widening circle of acquaintances, his sense of importance, the growing pressure of absorbing and agreeable work build up a sense of being really at home on earth. The young are generally less unwilling to die than the middle-aged and the old. 'Seventy years is not a day too much', says Screwtape, 'for the difficult task of unravelling their souls from heaven and building up a firm attachment to the earth.' All this is true and I can recognise in myself every item in Screwtape's hellish inventory of temptations for the middle-aged and elderly. Is it for this that I have been kept alive, despite so often putting myself (and always others) at hazard? Is Heaven further from me than it was in childhood? Is Priestland right about the sea?

With these thoughts in mind I now address some of the questions which form the framework of this book, concerning the feelings which I have about my own death, although I have spent a minimal amount of time and mental energy brooding upon it. There can be no doubt that where the prospect of death is concerned the Christian tradition is heavily loaded with fear. 'Fear death?' says Browning in 'Prospice', 'to feel the fog in my throat, the mist in my face.' This is fear, perhaps, of the

25

animal act of dying, natural enough. But the literature goes far beyond this. Psalm 49:14 says of the dead:

> they lie in the hell like sheep,
> death *gnaweth* upon them.

Shakespeare stages a debate on the subject in *Measure for Measure*, III.i. where the Duke of Vienna bids Claudio 'Be absolute for death', and the latter, who unlike the Duke is actually confronting death, memorably demurs:

> *To lie in cold obstruction and to rot; . . .*
> *To be imprison'd in the viewless winds, . . .*
> *. . . or to be worse than worst*
> *Of those that lawless and incertain thoughts*
> *Imagine howling! – 't is too horrible!*

And there is no more chilling evocation of the fear of death than the chorus in T. S. Eliot's *Murder in the Cathedral*, II.i.:

> *. . . only is here*
> *The white flat face of Death, God's silent servant,*
> *And behind the face of Death the Judgement*
> *And behind the Judgement the Void, more horrid than*
> *active shapes of hell;*
> *Emptiness, absence, separation from God; . . .*
> *Where the soul is no longer deceived for there are no*
> *objects, no tones, . . .*
> *From seeing itself, foully united forever, nothing with*
> *nothing,*
> *Not what we call death, but what beyond death is*
> *not death,*
> *We fear, we fear.*

All this I read, recited and in the last case learned at school. It must have had its effect.

But fear, like pain, once it has lifted is soon forgotten. Also it takes time to build up, and in almost all the episodes where I have confronted death, there simply has not been time to feel afraid. The one exception was the Fastnet storm, and even then fear only came when the worst was over and we heard on the radio how much damage had been caused to the rest of the fleet. I had a pang of remorse at having brought youngsters, including one of my own sons, into this precarious place. But the need to reassure the young crew soon allayed it.

I do, however, suffer from fear of flying, particularly in helicopters when flying high. This is quite irrational, since when closer to the ground one is actually less safe; there can be too little time to cope with an emergency. Only on one occasion has anything like this actually happened. The fan-belt broke on a small helicopter in which I was travelling, but the pilot (Patrick Lort Phillips) shut down the engine and landed the aircraft without bending so much as a blade of corn, so I cannot count that among my brushes with eternity. There is more time for apprehension when travelling by airliner, particularly before take-off and on landing. In almost none of the emergencies that I have spoken of did prayer play any part. But I do habitually launch arrow prayers (normally 'Our Father . . .') at the beginning and end of airline flights. It is easy to scoff at this, as merely seeking a bit of supernatural 'lift' at critical moments, but I do not think of these prayers like that. If I am to die, and since there is nothing whatever I can do about it, let me at least be praying – the highest activity of which I can be capable. And if the thing does crash then there is more chance of my acting responsibly, rather than just to save my own skin, if I have a prayer on my lips when it occurs.

But the fear, in the passages quoted above, is less of dying than of what 'beyond death is not death' – the prospect of some afterlife. How realistic is this? Traditional Christian teaching seems to say clearly that the soul, freed from its mortal body at death, will be incarnated in a new and glorified 'body' at the Resurrection, when Christ himself comes again in Glory. The way that the New Testament hammers away at the need to *believe* both in Christ's saving power and in the reality of His Resurrection, shows that it was as hard to swallow this in the first century as it is today. My wife has suffered from a congenital abnormality of the blood vessels in her brain, which eventually had the effect of short-circuiting the blood supply away from the higher centres. As the condition progressed, over a period of a few months, I had the agonising experience of seeing her slipping away from me into the wholly unreal world of pre-senile dementia. Once the neurones, for want of oxygen, cease to fire, neither reason, perception, memory nor personality can function. When admitted to the National Hospital for Nervous Diseases she had no measurable IQ. By means of an insertion through a blood vessel, blobs of glue were positioned to close off the short-circuit and her mind returned more or less undamaged. She is the same person that I love, and all her old memories are intact. But after death there is no more brain; the structure crumbles and the molecules dissipate. Once the neurones have gone, with the information stored in them and the rich pattern of their interconnections, in what sense can the personality persist? In modern terms the 'software' of the human personality cannot exist nakedly *in vacuo*. Where and in what 'hardware' can this information be carried: how, even 'in Christ', can it be resurrected? No one has attempted an answer to these questions, relying on simple faith and embroidering the outcome.

28

But even the embroidery contains major difficulties, not only because of the all too vivid reality of Hell in the Christian imagination but more because of the insipidity of most of what passes for Heaven. The almost universal Christian depiction of Heaven is as a state of peace. This is not even the Hebrew peace, *shalom*, the busy prosperity of the godly city, but the Latin peace, *pax*, the absence of war and the end of striving. *Requiescat in pace.* But it is precisely in the striving that personality comes to full flowering. Browning wrote much about Heaven and underlined this point in the poem entitled 'Andrea del Sarto (called the "faultless painter")':

> ... *all is silver grey*
> *Placid and perfect with my art – the worst!*
> *Ah, but a man's reach should exceed his grasp*
> *Or what's a Heaven for?*

Yet it is hard to devise a Heaven, even in the imagination, which is not silver grey. If it is full of striving, who are we striving against (not all can be winners) and what are we striving for?

Bishop Richard Harries, in his recent book *Christ is Risen* (Mowbrays) recognises that for the individual human being there is no satisfactory answer to these problems. At death, he says, we may go out into the dark and know nothing. But God continues to know us. 'Our knowledge may cease but God does not forget us; and this essential self he clothes with a means of expression appropriate to eternity' (page 115). It is hard to know what this might mean. Sheila Cassidy, the doctor tortured by the Pinochet regime in Santiago and now running a hospice near Plymouth, puts the same point in more vivid language. In an interview on Radio 4 I heard her say: 'Even the cleverest theologian does not know that there is a life after death. I say to my patients, "It may after all be only a long sleep. But it just might be something so bloody marvellous that we shall all be asking ourselves what on earth we have been making all that fuss about." ' She ignores, and I suppose she has every right to do so, the Christian prospect of a place of torment. But so, I guess, do most of us.

I have no problem about agnosticism as to the fact or falsehood of immortality. Austin Farrer, the Oxford theologian, found it bleak and believed that there is no consolation which carries any force other than the promise of an invisible and an eternal good. But C. S. Lewis could never see how a preoccupation with that subject at the outset could fail to corrupt the whole thing. I find his attitude the more appealing. It has the merit of focusing our attention upon this life as being all that we are sure of, and if we wish to live well (whatever that may mean) it is no use storing up goodies against a future existence which may never materialise.

Another mistake is to set too much store on what we can hand on to successors. It is hard that my father-in-law, who worked impossible hours at his medical practice throughout the war at great cost to his health, then sold it to a man who ran it down and soon went out of business. But the good my father-in-law had done was its own reward, and he had no right to look for any other. It is hard when a man's sons have no aptitude for the business he has built up for them. But every man or woman's life is of limitless value, so Christ teaches us, within its own span and on its own terms. What we can or cannot hand on is out of our control, and it is fruitless to worry too much about it.

As I move into the late afternoon of life I find myself more and more concerned not to be a nuisance to other people. It is possible, and one sees it often, that even with

the mind still active, there can be a clear sense that bodily
infirmity, failing energies or even simple disillusionment
makes life no longer any fun. When people have the sense
of being no use, either to themselves or those around
them, they feel it is time to move on – and often say
so. 'God can take me at any time . . . I wish He would
get on with it.' There is no wickedness in this, nor even
selfishness; it is simply to take a realistic view of one's
own good and that of others. But suicide has a bitter
flavour and euthanasia even worse, for good reasons. If
doctors were licensed to put people down at their own
request there would have to be elaborate safeguards
and certification. What is to prevent the family, very
much against her real will, putting pressure on Aunt
Sophie to agree to the procedure? It will save so much
money in medical bills, free the house, and exonerate
the family from visiting at weekends which is really
rather a torment for all concerned. The blood curdles.
Doctors now, in a secret compact with patients, slip in
an overdose when the pain gets too intense and certify a
death by natural causes. Thank God that they do so. But
Heaven forbid that this ever becomes formalised. Meanwhile, I can only pray that, well before that time comes,
He will have called my number in. Keats, an apothecary
by training, wrote his 'Ode to a Nightingale' a year or so
before dying of consumption at the age of twenty-five. He
calls the bird 'immortal' which is a bit far-fetched, but of
himself he confesses:

> *Darkling I listen; and for many a time*
> *I have been half in love with easeful Death,*
> *Called him soft names in many a musèd rhyme,*
> *To take into the air my quiet breath;*
> *Now more than ever seems it rich to die,*
> *To cease upon the midnight with no pain . . .*

31

Perhaps, when it comes to the point, I would sooner be listening to Mozart than a nightingale, but to cease upon the midnight with no pain is something I can surely pray for.

My wife who, in addition to her cranial problems, has lost both breasts to cancer, suffers from a deep-vein thrombosis in one leg and much arthritis, talks a lot about her impending death in a very matter-of-fact manner. Our children find this disconcerting but the grandchildren take it for granted. As a medical person no longer able to practise, she sees it as part of her vocation to talk to people freely about disease and death, without ever forcing the conversation. For some people this undoubtedly is helpful, bringing the subject down to earth and exorcising fear. Others, no doubt, would sooner not know. I find this freedom of conversation very helpful in facing the prospect of losing her, while remembering that there is no way of knowing which of us will go first.

When the time comes, if indeed it does, for either of us to go through the dark valleys of pain and fear, intensive nursing, dressings, drips and scans, loss of sense or consciousness and then the last word of parting, one can only hope to hang on to the thought that God will still be with us; that within the reality of the Body of Christ, crucified, risen, glorified, we can find the means to trust that God is present and active in the very processes of disintegration. Today I hardly know what those words mean. But I strive to follow the path of St Francis. In 1225, when Francis had been brought to Assisi, wounded, virtually blind and in great pain, he wrote his 'Canticle of the Sun', the first great poem in the Italian language. It is a paean of praise to God, the essence of human and more than human gladness. In the third from last stanza it says:

All praise be yours, my Lord, through Sister Death,
From whose embrace no mortal can escape.
Woe to those who die in mortal sin!
Happy are those She finds doing your will!
The second death can do no harm to them.

I hope that when that time comes I can be as courteous
as St Francis was to Sister Death, and I hope she will find
me in a good disposition. As for the second death this can
only refer to what T. S. Eliot described as 'what beyond
death is not death, . . . foully united forever, nothing
with nothing'. From this, the final horror of separation,
may the Good Lord deliver me. I had better stick close
by Him meanwhile, in case I am taken by surprise.

In the sandwich bar where I often lunch there is
a new sweet on sale called 'Death by Chocolate'. It is
spongy, rich and delicious. There might be worse ways
of going.

(Estelle Beach died a few months after this contribution
was completed.)

DEATH, A DARK
IMMACULATE FLOWER

Saba Risaluddin

Saba Risaluddin is a European (English father, Swiss mother) born in England and educated partly in England and partly in Switzerland. After graduating from Lausanne University in 1963, she tried a variety of careers before settling, ten or fifteen years later, to just two in tandem: writing, and running her own independent financial advisory company, through which she is introducing financial products designed especially for Muslims (she became a Muslim in 1986). Drawing on her experience in creating and restoring gardens (among others on behalf of the National Trust), she is the author of several books on plants and gardening. With her present husband, she is the creator of the Calamus Foundation, an organisation devoted to promoting harmony between adherents of the Abrahamic faiths by emphasising their common heritage.

The religious influences that shaped my early life were unemphatic, all in shades of grey with never a clear-cut, black-and-white opinion anywhere: on the one hand, an Anglican father who scarcely ever entered a church; on the other, a slightly disapproving Calvinist mother – disapproving, that is, even of the token remnants of Papism that lingered in the services we occasionally endured in the little country church where spirituality seemed to vanish with the entry of the vicar and congregation.

On my mother's side of the family, Switzerland seemed to be peopled almost entirely with aunts and cousins, a beloved grandmother and her sisters of great age. If a great-aunt dared to think of dying before reaching her nineties, she was frowned upon for letting the family down, and in some curious way this longevity rubbed off on the great-uncles' wives, so that there was an ample supply of sprightly widows in the family. (Men, being regarded as the weaker vessels, were exempt from the requirement to live long.)

For all that, in so large a family, where regular reunions were held, death was ever present, in a way that would have been perhaps more familiar to a child of a hundred years ago than to one born almost at the end of the 1939–45 war. Funerals were followed by a gathering of the family at which everyone had a good time, celebrating a life rather than mourning a death. Not for us the coy evasions of 'He has passed away'; though few of the family would have read Rebecca Richmond's poem that begins 'Death is a clean bold word', all would have agreed with her

. . . nor say your lover, friend, your child
Has 'gone' as though he'd wandered off somewhere,
But speak with dignity and say 'He died'.

This ordered procession of lives from birth to death was hideously interrupted when I was fourteen by the suicide of my cousin, a brilliant but highly strung boy who was thrown over by his girlfriend just before his university finals. My uncle, a deeply sensitive, painfully reticent man, suffered as I hope never to see anyone suffer again. Only music, and the love of God, helped him

35

to endure; that, and his little daughter. The pain lay in loss, of course; but more than that, perhaps, in the sense of order violated, hopes and expectations destroyed.

Some of the deaths that are in the normal order of things touch one more nearly, of course. My father, another *grand sensible* whose life had been traversed by the pain of loss and touched with the bitterness of youthful humiliations, talked much of death towards the end of his life. There was a sense of life weighing more heavily upon him than he could bear; he could no longer, in Sidney Keyes's words, 'muster the shards of pain to harmony', and he wanted an end of it. When the end came, I believed it brought him peace; I knew it brought me, his youngest child, inward winter.

During the years of my twenties, I suppose my attitudes towards death took much the form they still have, very little modified by my embracing another faith, Islam, some five years ago. Death itself holds no terrors, though the manner of dying certainly does, especially the slow humiliation of modern senescence. I find it hard to condemn the cottager my father told me about, one of those for whom, in the years before 1914, his first mother-in-law (who was also his aunt) held herself responsible. The old woman helped her bedridden, senile husband to leave this life after devotedly caring for him for years. 'I set him up in bed, ma'am, and I put a string round his neck and pulled, and he went off lovely.'

Having a hunger for knowledge, and a sense that huge things lie just beyond my comprehension, I look forward to death as the first step into an entirely new dimension. One of the books that influenced me as a child was J. W. Dunne's *An Experiment with Time*. He wrote, 'We must live together before we can attain to either intelligence or control at all. We must sleep if we are not to find ourselves, at death, helplessly strange to the new conditions. And we must die before we can hope to advance to a broader understanding.'

I have no difficulty in accepting that whatever we attempt to discover in this life is limited by, has to be interpreted through, our puny physical apprehension, so that much of what we read in the Qur'an, for example, is made clear to us through metaphor, adjusted to our narrow understanding. Another writer who influenced me in my teens was the now unfashionable Charles Morgan, who wrote that 'death, in its creative meaning, [was] impossible, as long as it was attached to the ideas of cessation and power ... but ... it was in the power of one dying to abrogate the idea of this body's decay and, being detached from the fleshly circumstance of death, to advance into perception' (Sparkenbroke, IV, 5).

Does human creativity derive only from the brain cells that will die with the body? Even the most transcendentally creative among us has not a limitless capacity of imagination, and for ordinary people like myself, things of the spirit have to be reached for through analogy. One person may wish to believe literally in the fragrant gardens, cooling rivers and sheltering trees of the Qur'anic paradise; another may take them as a metaphor for the divine love that we may hope to merit, and which we may, if deserving, apprehend more fully after death.

Hell, by contrast – described in the Qur'an in metaphors of fire, burning and scalding, of crushing pressures and of the abyss – stands for the denial of God and the terrible deprivation of His love. There is always before me the shadow of fear, which some no doubt would call conscience, that I may not be à la hauteur, may not be admitted to the halls of learning in the next life but will be instead cast into the deserts of ignorance. That would be hell indeed. Or do we get, after death, as some suggest, what we believe in – paradise, or hell, or le néant?

37

The Qur'an is quite clear on the matter: the death of the body is in the natural order of things, at a time appointed by God. At the Day of Judgment, also called the Day of Resurrection, every soul will be called to account and will be requited in full for former deeds. Life on this earth is not to be despised, as it seems to be in some strands of Christianity, but it is the cultivating ground for the life hereafter. Live life well on this earth, doing good to others, acquiring knowledge from the vast cumulative store laid down by mankind, neither disdaining nor worshipping the earthly benefits that God grants us, and do all this as a preparation for the perpetual life to come.

As a Muslim, I believe that the Qur'an is the revealed word of God, and as such it has a transcendence that no human creation can aspire to. Yet the poets and musicians, mathematicians and scientists, in exercising their human faculties of perception and imagination, can announce that transcendence.

When people who have had a near-death experience – including my previous husband, who finally died ten years later – speak of the tunnel of light, the glory that beckons them on, are they influenced by the folklore of death, by what they expect to experience? Is this a cultural phenomenon, in short, or a universal one? Assuming it to be a primary experience, clearly we cannot know until we experience it ourselves what lies at the end of the tunnel in the embrace of the welcoming light.

An old family friend told me how, soon after her husband died, she was alone and grieving, and cried out in her pain, 'Sam, Sam, where are you?' She distinctly heard his voice telling her, 'Don't be sad, I'm busy learning.' This unexpected response gave her great comfort, at least in part because it suggested that the individuality of the man she had loved lived on, and would not depend upon the memories she and others had of him for its eternal existence.

We owe our dread of another's death to that person's individuality: the fact of its being, and the fear of its loss. 'In the one word identity are involved perhaps the deepest and certainly the dearest human things,' wrote G. K. Chesterton in 'The Romance of Rhyme' (*Fancies versus Fads*, 1923). And Antoine de Saint-Exupéry believed that, '*Il n'est qu'un luxe véritable, et c'est celui de relations humaines*' (*Terre des Hommes*, chapter 2). But is the benediction of human relations confined only to this world? If our individuality survives at all after death, do our souls enjoy spiritual relationships with each other as well as with God? Is Rupert Brooke's 'most individual and bewildering ghost' ('Oh! Death will find me!', 1909) just a delusion?

The anticipation of reunion in another life has undoubtedly given immense comfort to many bereaved people. But another uncle of mine, who died a painful death of cancer of the spine, clung tightly to the belief that after death, each individual's soul loses its particularity and returns to a kind of central pool of soul-material, rather as a speck of mercury, dropped into a vat of the same metal, ceases to be an identifiable globule and becomes an indistinguishable part of the liquid mass. If that is so, why are we given such individuality for the time we spend in the shell of our body? Is that individuality really only composed of neurons and memory traces, of experiences endured and knowledge acquired only on this earth? Once the cells that form the brain have ceased to function, once the mind can no longer attempt to break out of its own confines, striving to reach an understanding of its own processes, is what we call our soul also gone? Or is it one of those huge things tantalisingly just out of reach of our earthly comprehension?

39

Some people have difficulty with the apparent contradiction between free will and predestination. Nothing can, ultimately, oppose the will of God, who is all-knowing; but mankind has the gift of free will, is able to make choices and decisions. We can choose, therefore, to live our lives as a preparation for the life to come; or we can choose to ignore what lies ahead and live only for the day. To that extent, the choice is ours between paradise and hell. And to that extent, also, death itself need not be feared, though the manner of its coming is a legitimate cause of apprehension.

The anticipation of a wondrous expansion of our limited understanding is also cause for a longing for death, which need not imply a rejection of God's blessings on this earth. A will to death, in these terms, is a will to transcendence. Ibn al-Arif (*d.c.* 1141 CE), a Sufi in muslim Spain who founded a new *tariqa* or 'school', said that, 'there are those to whom death is as a draught of pure water to the thirsty', and al-Ghazali, the great Islamic philosopher of the eleventh century CE, wrote of those who at death are separated from all that is not God. The one who dies 'rejoices that the obstacles which kept him from [the invocation of the Divine Name] have been removed, so that he finds himself alone with his Beloved'.

To judge from the stereotypes presented by the western media, Islam would appear to be in violent and often bigoted opposition to the Judaeo-Christian tradition that is the chief strand in a European upbringing and education. This is a narrow and misconceived perception of a faith which shares many of the traditions of both Judaism and Christianity; all three recognise Abraham, the first to grasp the one-ness of God, as their spiritual father; the moral values which underlie the three faiths are the same; all three (but especially Judaism and Islam) place great emphasis on a revealed book and upon the textual traditions that man has elaborated from the revelation. Simply, this means that I had no difficulty in accepting Islam, had no need to do violence to any of the mental baggage that a European upbringing has left me with, for the bits I was uncomfortable with – the divinity of Jesus, the Trinity, the priestly hierarchy – had all fallen away before I became a Muslim. Islam has given me greater peace of mind than I had before. But it has not enabled me to contemplate with equanimity the prospect of the death of those I love. It is one thing to imagine, as I quite often do, one's own death; quite another to prefigure the sense of pain and loss that must be endured after the death of another. This suggests to me that I am a good deal more selfish than I should like to think, or that I am deluding myself. I do not go so far as to agree with T. E. Lawrence, who wrote, 'Perhaps all physical existence is a weary pain to man; only by day his alert stubborn spirit will not acknowledge it.' But I do believe that we have it in us to ensure that the next life is a better one. And that being so, how can I legitimately grieve when someone I love attains that better state?

The moment I was told of the death of my previous husband, I said, 'Thank God.' His last months had indeed been a weary pain, and the sense of relief was immediate. But then, in the weeks that followed, I had to face my own shortcomings that had contributed to his suffering. Guilt is also a kind of grieving.

Some people, in times of loss, rail against God's injustice but most believers, I think, find comfort in their faith. Both the sense of grief and the consolation seem to transcend differences of dogma: the bereaved are united in their common humanity. Few Christians, though they have before them the example of Jesus himself, can bring themselves wholly to renounce this world's affections. Jesus, a Jew, dismissed in a few words

41

the family obligations that are considered sacred to Jews (another area of common ground with Muslims, for whom family and other human relations are formalised in the Qur'an), when he said, 'If anyone comes to me and does not hate his own father and mother and wife and children and brothers and sisters, yes, and even his own life, he cannot be my disciple' (Luke 14:26).

As Muslims, we are guided to the middle path, saluting the unique value of each human being, yet setting even the dearest human relations in the context of an eternal, all-merciful and all-forgiving God, so that death becomes a necessary loss in this life, opening the way to the next. In this, as in all other aspects of our faith, God's mercy is upon us: 'He has laid no hardship upon you in religion' (Surah 22, *The Pilgrimage*: 78).

DARK REFLECTIONS

Professor Stewart R. Sutherland,
Vice-Chancellor, University of London

*A Scot by birth, Stewart Sutherland was educated first
at the University of Aberdeen, then at Corpus Christi College, Cambridge. After several years teaching philosophy
in Wales and Scotland, he became Professor of the History
and Philosophy of Religion at King's College, London.
Between 1985 and 1990 he was Principal of the College,
a post he relinquished when becoming Vice-Chancellor of
the University of London in September 1990. He has wide
interests, especially in the field of religion and philosophy
and, amongst other topics, has written on 'Atheism and
the Rejection of God', and 'Faith and Ambiguity'. He is
married with one son and two daughters.*

I

Then t' worms 'll coom an' eat thee up.

I do not think that I had a particularly macabre early
education, but that line from 'Ilkley Moor' set, of course,
alongside all the other more usual specimens of the 'All
things bright and beautiful' type, is one tiny but significant inhabitant of the satchel full of ideas, emotions and
memories with which I moved from primary to secondary
school. At one level, perhaps, the blunt (calling-a-spade-
a-bloody-shovel variety of) Yorkshire sentiment had a
certain appeal to that streak of gallows-humour to be

found in parts of Scotland, but it had the advantage of signposting, almost before we were aware of it, the collusion in the natural world between life and death.

That death is part of the natural order of things is a truth which, however we rail, rage and rant, will not go away. To say this is not to fail to be moved by Dylan Thomas's exhortation to his chronically ill father, 'Do not go gentle into that good night', but it is to raise a question about the point or direction of the anger. Nature makes no bargains with us; nature breaks no promises. Rather we collude with that pattern of life and death by our very existence. Just as our descendants can live only if they do not have to compete with us for space, for food, for oxygen, so too we live on the chemistry of the death of others. The force of the anger of Thomas's poem to which I shall return does not deny that fact; it presupposes it. A sub-text of this essay will be the attempt to find the focus of the emotions, be they anger, fear, horror, rage or rebellion, which are provoked, or at least apparently so, by death. Perhaps the truth of the matter is that in contemplating death we become as children once again and rant and wail and stamp our feet because we wish it were not so. If that is the case then there is little more to be said, and all that is to be done is to find ways of sheltering ourselves from the truth about death, and disguising in polite society the truth about ourselves. Whether by accident or design, the gradual displacement, rather than replacement, of the rituals of death in our society seems to suggest that our culture is following such a route.

However, reality has its own corrective powers, and even if that were our inclination, there is a point at which matters are no longer in our hands and whether individually or culturally, the natural world imposes its own terms. Thus perhaps there is more to be said.

The issues confronting us are debated intermittently in various conversations reported by James Boswell in his *Life of Johnson* (OUP, 1980). Of one such occasion, Boswell wrote,

When we were alone, I introduced the subject of death and endeavoured to maintain that the fear of it might be got over. I told him that David Hume said to me he was no more uneasy to think he should *not be* after life, than that he *had not been* before he began to exist.

Johnson reacted strongly, having no higher opinion of Hume's views on this than on most other matters: 'Sir, if he really thinks so, his perceptions are disturbed; he is mad: if he does not think so, he lies.' Johnson was, however, too precipitate, and indeed was so aroused by Boswell's attempt to keep the conversation going that he dismissed his friend, adding unusually, 'Don't let us meet tomorrow' (ibid. p.427). The question implied by Hume's reported claim is a fair one and will provide us with a sharp focus for the next stage of the discussion: if we are not distressed by the thought that once we were not, that before birth we did not exist, why should the thought that in due course (after death) we will not be, will no longer exist, be a source of dread or anxiety?

A related point was, according to Boswell, put to Johnson many years later by a Miss Seward 'the poetess of Lichfield': 'There is one mode of the fear of death, which is certainly absurd; and that is the dread of annihilation, which is only a pleasing sleep without a dream.' (ibid. p. 950)

Johnson had two points of reply:

It is neither pleasing, nor sleep; it is nothing. Now mere existence is so much better than nothing, that one would rather exist even in pain, than not exist. (ibid.)

The lady confounds annihilation, which is nothing, with the apprehension of it, which is dreadful. It is in the apprehension of it that the horror of annihilation consists. (ibid. p. 951)

When the contentious name of Hume is absent, Johnson begins to argue and these exchanges clarify some of the central questions which I wish to address. (For the record, however, it should be noted that much of Johnson's fear of death (as distinct from annihilation) was grounded in his lively belief in Hell, in judgement after death and in his own unworthiness.)

II

The question which, in his dispute with both Hume and Miss Seward, Johnson forces upon us, is whether to exist, to be alive, is *always* better than death or annihilation. If it is, and if there is no 'after life', then we are miserable creatures indeed for things are bound to get worse. Hence for many, the importance of belief in life beyond the grave, for only then can they avoid the belief that we shall be deprived of what is of highest or ultimate value.

Such an interplay of belief gives coherent contest to both Johnson on the one hand, and Dylan Thomas's rage against death on the other. If there is no life to come, then what can we do but defy or dread death, knowing all the while that our fate is inevitable and our feelings no defence against grim realities? Those who believe in a benevolent form of life beyond death can avoid such apparently desperate straits, but what of those who do not have such certainty? Must they simply avoid thinking about such things?

I want in a modest and moderate way to argue that such a view of the options is too constrained, too limited. The difference, I shall suggest, is the difference between, on the one hand, regarding death as a glass through which we see darkly, and on the other, finding death to be a mirror, which reflects what is real in this life.

In the former case, we have limited beliefs about and perceptions of what lies beyond this life. Such a view sets limits to what we value in this life for it implies a greater perhaps even perfect world elsewhere. What can follow from this is a life-denying set of beliefs which distracts from what is of deep value in this life. Alternatively, and at the other end of a wide spectrum, it can point pictures of such a future life filled with the trivia of this life, but endlessly so. These dangers are there quite apart from the problems of providing good grounds for such a belief or set of beliefs.

The alternative picture of death as a mirror is worth consideration for it is a way of representing to ourselves the fact that whether through obituaries, eulogies spoken at funerals or memorial services, or whether simply in the still dark hours of grief, death is perhaps more than anything else the occasion of deep and profound reflection upon this life. The ambiguity of the word 'reflective' here is both fortuitous and instructive. Death forces us to re-evaluate life. The prospect of death might be a source of self-instruction or self-knowledge rather than despair or fear. On this view, it is the case perhaps that in exhorting his father not to 'go gently' Thomas's rage is not against death, but rage about the life which was thus ebbing away. If we pass this way but once, then more important than ever is the nature or quality of the journey.

The most fundamental issue raised by death is whether survival is the most important thing in life. Bishop Butler once claimed that the most important question in this life is whether there is some future world. That implies in Johnsonian fashion that what we value most is existence (I am tempted to add 'mere' existence). There is an alternative view, but I want at the outset to state very clearly that in seeking such an alternative I do not in any way wish to devalue existence or, more properly, individual life. I am not, that is to say, pursuing a path which denies value to individual existence and *ipso facto* to the individual. Quite to the contrary I hope that I shall be giving an account of *some* of the reasons for the value which we do attach to individual human life.

Let Socrates be our example. In the accounts of Socrates' trial and the short period of life remaining to him after that, Plato explores in a variety of ways the relationship between life and death in Socrates' thought. Socrates had been sentenced to death on the charge of corrupting the youth of Athens. His defence was essentially that he taught those who would listen no more and no less than to seek after truth and to pursue this as the most important goal of life.

Inevitably, of course, this meant unmasking claims to knowledge and certainty in others which were ill-founded. Negatively that is a short way to unpopularity. Positively Socrates taught that what is of ultimate value is knowledge and that all knowledge must be built upon self-knowledge. Only through self-knowledge could we be aware of our own ignorance, and only then could we find a starting point for knowledge rather than opinion.

In his trial Socrates pointed out that if the charge of 'corrupting the youth' was a charge against teaching

48

the fundamental importance of self-knowledge, then he must plead 'guilty'. Of course, his defence was that, in fact, this was quite the contrary to corrupting the youth. Doubtless there were those in this citizens' court who might have wished that some way out of this situation could be found, before the otherwise inevitable sentence of death was imposed.

The irony of the situation was such that any 'way out' other than withdrawing the charges would have involved Socrates in denying what was the whole *rationale* of his life: that truth and self-knowledge are of ultimate value. Plea-bargaining was not on the agenda. Not even the 'civilised' form which the death penalty took in Athens – the self-inflicted death of drinking the due dose of hemlock – could moderate the starkness of choices available to Socrates on the one hand and the court on the other.

Death was the mirror which faced both the judges and the accused. To execute this individual was to reveal something deep and subversive of truth in Athenian society. On Socrates' part, to share in the compromise of finding a way out of the difficulty would be to deny that truth and self-knowledge are ultimately of greater value than mere existence. This applies both to himself and to the court which was to sentence him to death. This is an extremely important point.

It could be argued that he could have satisfied the crucial claims of self-knowledge in this fearful situation by discovering something about himself which is doubtless true of the most of the rest of us: namely, that he was more afraid of death than courageous in the cause of truth and that therefore he would give the court (false) grounds on which they could acquit him. That surely is self-knowledge. The point being missed, however, is that in such a manoeuvre one forgets that death is the mirror here not only to the accused, but to the accusers. For the latter self-knowledge is made possible only by forcing the issue. The question of what is true about Athenian society is only resolved if the *court* has to make the stark choice between 'guilty' and 'not guilty', between life and death. And, of course, only Socrates could provoke that choice by refusing to temporise. Death and the power to inflict it by judicial process was the mirror which Socrates held up to Athens.

In fact he was sentenced to death and a further act was added to the drama. His friends and disciples reacted as good and courageous friends might and they plotted an escape for Socrates from the condemned cell. A boat would be standing by and he would be taken to safety beyond the jurisdiction of Athens. He would be free once again to teach, and to teach others the ultimate value of truth and self-knowledge. How marvellous to have such friends. Perhaps a happy ending would be possible after all. The mirror of death had been held up for both accused and accuser to contemplate: the integrity of Socrates was not at issue and yet by this plot his life might also be preserved.

The friends, however, had not fully reckoned with Socrates. Perhaps they had not fully understood what, indirectly by question rather than answer, he had taught. He did not question their courage or their love for him, but he did refuse to escape. The grounds were simple and the logic was impeccable. To flee now would be to show that ultimately there was something of greater value than truth and self-knowledge. In choosing what we might call 'life' or 'existence' or even 'mere existence', he would be stating that the greatest harm which could befall a man or woman was the loss of life rather than the loss of truth and integrity.

Whether we agree with Socrates on the *specific* decision taken is not the primary issue. I must confess to a sneaking feeling that there were one or two additional arguments which I should have wanted Socrates' friends to put to him in the condemned cell. The point at issue, however, is to illustrate what I mean by my view of death as a mirror we darkly see. Death in this sense forces us to reconsider what is of ultimate value in this life. This is not simply a version of the idea of the recording angel who will embarrass and shame us with a catalogue of our evasions and inadequacies. Such a picture may be a threat necessary to give backbone to our weak and wayward wills, but it is a much too simplistic picture to give us deep insight into the complex moral structures of human life.

The recording angel presupposes total agreement and some knowledge of what should be recorded. There is no need for reflection in either sense of the word for we already know what is expected of us and it is simply a matter of doing it!

If this were the whole story, then death would be by no means a mirror: it would be, for most of us, simply the doorway to the attic in which stands a personalised version of the portrait of Dorian Gray. The picture of death as a mirror carries with it the full ambiguity of the term 'reflection'. It turns us back on life both in terms of what we see and how we understand what we see.

III

In the fairy tale, the Wicked Queen addresses the mirror thus:

Mirror, mirror on the wall,
Who is the fairest of them all?

The reply, of course, is not the one that is wanted, but the story makes clear a number of fundamental points about the connection between mirrors and reality. There is application of all of these points to the idea of death as a mirror.

The most distinctive thing about a mirror is that it gives us an alternative view of ourselves and our place in the world. We discover through mirrors the possibility of a different vantage point upon ourselves. As we know from the story of Narcissus this does not automatically prevent self-absorption, but it does imply the distinction between the way things are and the way we might want them to be. As I look in the mirror I cannot believe that I am either Cary Grant or Quasimodo, however much I may want to dramatise myself, any more than the Queen could believe that she was more beautiful than Snow White.

Death is the type of mirror which sets limits to the illusion in my life, and here the word 'illusion' is used in the precise Freudian sense of what I *wish* to be true. The whole force of the line quoted at the outset of this essay,

Then t'worms 'll coom an' eat thee up

is to strip us of illusion and its near neighbour, pretence. Death sets limits to illusion in the most dramatic of ways: it sets limits to life. However, the very same power of death to strip us of illusion is that power which points to the possibility of alternative views of ourselves and that is the precondition of there being such a goal as self-knowledge. A tree cannot have self-knowledge for the same reason that a tree cannot look into a mirror; not, that is, for the contingent reason that it has no eyes, but because there is no possibility of reflection even in the sense provoked by the metaphorical mirror of extinction or death.

The difference between the mirror which is death and other literal or even metaphorical mirrors, is profound. The mirror of death is the conditional and therefore the source of our knowledge of our own finitude or temporality. The most fundamental lesson we learn about ourselves is our finitude, and the surest, most uncompromising, teacher is death. We are not self-sufficient, in the sense of independent, in what lies outside of us. Death is the final proof of that.

Fortunately, however, although that may be the single most important truth about the human condition, it is not the only truth about the human condition. Death, in setting limits to life, tells us of our finitude, but it equally poses the question of the eternal. To have the conception of finitude is to have the conception of the transcendence of that finitude. Just as one cannot have the concept of darkness without the concept of light – for they are mutually inter-dependent ideas – so to have the conception of our own finitude is to have the conception of the possibility of what is eternal, or transcendent.

Socrates had a knowledge of himself as subject to death, but he can also be understood in such a way that in accepting death he transcended that death. That is to say, in choosing not to evade the sentence, nor its implications, he demonstrated that there was in his life something which could not be taken from him by death, something more important than 'mere existence'. That is something to be seen reflected in the mirror which is death.

DEATH, BE NOT PROUD ...
A REFLECTION ON PEACE
AT THE LAST

James O'Connell, Professor of Peace Studies,
University of Bradford

*James O'Connell has been Professor of Peace Studies at
the University of Bradford since 1978. This followed an
academic career which took him from Professor of Government at Ahmadu Bello University to Professor of Politics
at the University of Ibadan, both in Nigeria, to Professor
and Dean of the Faculty of Arts at Ulster College, in the
Northern Ireland Polytechnic. His interests are in peace
education, disarmament and the politics of development,
and he has published widely in these fields.*

Recently somebody was telling me about an old woman
whom she knew. The old woman wanted to die but could
not; she had started to go completely blind, and she
was already deaf. I was wrung with sympathy for an
old person whose time had come but who was not able
to go. Her condition also touched a deep chord of fear
inside me. All my life I have been afraid of enclosed places,
terrified of rigid walls which might hold my head in their
vice and which could explode panic inside my body. The
old woman's blindness, laid on top of deafness, caused a
shiver of taut terror to run along my bones.

Death beckons through the indices of age. The first
irrefutable index of ageing came to me when I had to wear

spectacles with bifocal lenses. The short-sightedness of my youth was now compounded by the long-sightedness of middle age. Yet once middle age is recognised and assimilated, it is still possible to hope for a long, mature intellectual period that sets aside almost indefinitely the problems of physical decline and decay; and one can scale heights and stand on achievements that youth only glimpsed. In my own case middle age has been cut across by love and marriage and by the arrival of children. Without the children love might have caught the colours of an Indian summer, but with the children I am recalled from middle age into an earlier period. This recall process is threaded also with the company of strange young peers who are the other parents waiting at school doors for children as young as mine. Above all, the relentless importunings of my children hold back the psychological arrival of late middle age until I can no longer distinguish between those deficiencies of mine that stem from declining energies and those that belong to rigidities acquired by a temperament that from early on maintained a distance from other people, that leaned too much towards thinking and lived too often in dry leaves of paper.

Yet if I have been able to avoid in measure the problem of physical decline and have undergone the rejuvenating impact of children, I have not treated death as a spectre. I have kept death honestly in mind. In recent times, however, the prospect of dying has become for me a more vivid consciousness, partly because counting the years imposes on me a logic that it would be craven to hide from, partly also because relatives, friends and colleagues have died or have had heart attacks, and partly, finally, because now more than before, I sense a physical running down of my capacities.

What happens to people – or what has happened to

me – on going into later middle age is that they begin to realise that things will outlast them, even projects that they themselves are getting under way. Overall, this sense of being outlasted – which is run through by a sense of being on the way out – is overshadowed by the bomb: a threat to the existence of everyone, and not least a threat to the hope of the old, hope of achievement that is reborn in their hope for the young. In my case my children who would be the grandchildren of my peers prompt me to seek to stretch time. I am willing to die, and I ask God, 'Not yet', less for my sake than for those who need me. I suppose, too, that the peace issue which concerns me personally and professionally induces me also to look for more time. There are not enough persons concerned about peace, and those who are, are for that reason required to increase or multiply the effective moments of their time. Yet I also want to accept that God's will, not mine, be done in respect of the amount of time left to me.

The foregoing considerations are not those I set out to deal with initially in this short and impressionistic paper. They resemble more an undergrowth that is best cleared so that I can reach the tree which I want to cut down. Whether I meet death sooner or later, it can't be too far away. That is why I began to pen these lines and why I started with the entombing experience of the old lady which touches my phobias and threatens my mental defences.

If we accept death – especially if like Michelangelo its thought is sculpted on our hearts – there are probably three broad ways of dying that are tolerable for most of us. The first way is to die suddenly, without warning, swept into eternity with time being immediately suppressed and transmuted. It takes courage to make this choice of dying. It is to accept death now, in its immediacy, not seeking to eke out the dregs of life, not trying to savour its last lingering moments, and not being able to dispose of life's accumulations. Logically to welcome sudden death is to be ready for it, to have dealt with the procrastination that steals time from most of us, and to know that a sudden blow is the kindest cut.

The second way is to die lucidly over a period of time while being cared for and loved, not proving too great a burden, and being able to gather oneself for taking leave and for moving into eternity. Dying like that provides time for those who are left behind and time also for oneself to make a conscious gesture to God. It has its great burdens in the manner in which strength ebbs and in which the mind finds its resources growing desperately limited. But often that is only at the very end of dying.

The third way is to suffer a sharp and terminal illness that leaves one with time enough to bid good-bye and yet with a requirement to depart quickly. In some respects this manner of dying combines the most advantageous features of the first two.

I don't know if statistics exist on the manner in which people die. But I know enough from my own experience of watching people die to understand that there is a good chance of dying in a way different from the three ways I have set out. It is for that reason that I began to put these lines together, while I can. Apart from the many ways of dying that are possible, it is difficult to speculate about the manner of one's death. Even if death takes a form that one has pondered on, it will still be shaped by so many personal features and social circumstances that it makes more sense at this stage to realise that acceptance is more crucial than prevision. Nevertheless I want to spell out three broad ways of dying, each of which strikes fear into me and each of which I would like in some measure to anticipate, and through anticipating them – not in their detail which is futile, but in their broad possibilities – I want to try and die as humanly as I can.

Those three possible ways of dying that are full of fear for me are: dying from a stroke or in an accident that leaves me without wits for a long period before death; dying so painfully that my moral and physical resources cannot cope; and dying in such a way that trauma reaches into areas of the mind and body where my personal phobias operate. In the first kind of dying one is left an apparent vegetable and people can scarcely discern that there is still a spirit present and want to be released from waiting on the shell of a human person. In the second and painful kind of dying there is eventually less a leave-taking of loved ones and a sense of going to God than a pressure of pain that wears down personal energies and begs for merciful oblivion. In the third kind of dying that touches on phobic recesses of terror one might be, for example, left struggling for breath and reaching out excessively to stay alive, or stricken through a stroke that leaves one entombed in a body where the mind still works, where a hand still barely presses but where no words can pass through lips to let others know that there is still some residual urge to communicate.

Whichever way I am going to die I want to face the reality that I am going to die. I want to accept it now. Beyond that, I want to share my acceptance of death with those I love and among whom I hope to die. I want in the process to offer my acceptance of death to God, including the kind of death that will come to me; and I offer my death to God with the offering that Christ made to him for the whole world.

The assumption built into a will-to-accept-death in offering my life – that is, me and all I am and have done – to God as well as to those I love, is that my death forms

58

an integral part of my life and takes its quality from my life as a whole. I don't deny that even at the moment of death a new turning is not possible or that God cannot touch me in a new way. But even that human turning or divine touch can take place only within the continuity of my life and times.

I am offering my life, and I am accepting death now. I am doing so while I can, and while I have the resources. If I have time and energy and freedom at the end to make a final acceptance and offering, I hope to do so, and that will form part of the continuum of my life. But if I should not have the intellect, or if pain or phobia should obscure my basic will, I want now to affirm that I make knowingly in advance the gesture that is needed at the end as it is needed in principle at every moment of life. This is the heart of what I have set out to say in this document. Like fundamental human things, such as declaring love, it is greatly simple, no matter what complexity it comes out of or contains.

I had got this far in my reflections on dying when I realised that in working on my problem I had stumbled on the approach that Christ had worked out to the same problem. He could guess, and in measure could foresee, the agony of his dying. He was afraid of the chalice, wanted it to pass from him, but wanted his Father's will done. Christ made his final acceptance of death on the cross: 'Into your hands I commend my spirit.' But in the meal on the evening before, he formally accepted his death and declared his acceptance in ritual. On the following day the power of his executioners, the pain of scourging and crucifixion, the ugliness of the blood and dirt of his passion, the ebbing of his energy, the sense of having been abandoned that he could not conceal – all served to obscure how selflessly he accepted his Father's will and how fully he offered himself for those he loved.

The ritual offering of the Thursday night was not necessary to his sacrifice on Calvary. But it made clear that if death was being imposed on him he also took it on in fulfilment of his mission. The ritual of the bread and wine in his Last Supper brought out graphically and yet stated with serene gravity that he was freely offering his life. In asking his disciples also to go on enacting the same ritual he sought to keep his memory and presence among them, and he enabled them to join their offering of life and death to his. De la Taille, one of the greatest theologians of the Eucharist, summed up well in saying that the Last Supper was Calvary in anticipation and the Mass was Calvary in retrospect.

If I have recourse to a device used by Christ it only suggests how much like other people he was, 'in all things found as man'. I differ from him, however, as do other people, in carrying the weight of my sins with me to the grave. My sins diminish my offering and flaw my acceptance of mortality as they do my acceptance of God. Yet I believe in the forgiveness of sins as I do in life everlasting. Fortunately God has first loved us, including me, so though he needs my free offering to him as his love touches me and works through me, he takes me as I am. I don't have to – and I can't – merit him. He gives himself as a free gift. If in this context the thought of purgatory has any meaning, it simply represents God's love that in a final act of purification takes me into the infinite holiness of his good company.

I see through a glass darkly, and I remain afraid. I am afraid of death, and I am afraid of dying. I cannot see God's eternity clearly or understand how I will enter it. Mortal as I am I grieve for my mortality: 'the blight man was born for' (Gerard Manley Hopkins, 'Spring and Fall'). Yet my finite being has no meaning for me outside an understanding of God. In some obscure way his

60

presence is not only metaphysical reality in which I live and move and have my being but provides a salient dimension of my thinking. So I see in faith, walk in hope and seek to grow in love. Finally, while I have always in measure sought to offer God in the Eucharist all that I am and have, now as I grow older I offer him more consciously my death along with Christ's death. I cherish also more gladly the hope that is given by the risen Christ and that is rooted in God's eternal love.

ON CONTEMPLATING DEATH

Rabbi Dr Jonathan Magonet, Principal, Leo Baeck College

After Westminster School, Jonathan Magonet studied medicine and became a junior hospital doctor before training for the Rabbinate at Leo Baeck College in 1967. He returned to join the staff of the college in 1974 and became its principal in 1985. He is also Vice-president of the World Union for Progressive Judaism and plays a leading role in the development of improved understanding between Christians and Jews. Alongside maintaining his academic interest in biblical studies he has co-edited the Reform Synagogue's new Prayer Books. He and his wife Dorothea have a son and a daughter.

> *But I have reason to believe*
> *We all will be received in Graceland.*
> Paul Simon

This is a risky subject, not because of what it exposes of the writer, nor because of some superstition about what such contemplation may do to my own 'destiny', 'karma', 'luck' or other such mysterious magical process that needs to be appeased. I am relatively unsuperstitious about such matters – or at least agnostic, touch wood! Rather it is the risk of setting up a programme of heroic resignation, or pious detachment in the face of my own death, that will utterly fall apart when the actual crunch comes. Never make promises you are unlikely to keep – a healthy enough value for matters of relationships in this world, how much more appropriate for the time of parting. But then again, maybe consistency and precision are also straitjackets or idols of a certain kind. Who knows either the circumstances or one's own reaction, let alone one's ability still even to react? A car crash or a plug pulled on a chronically comatose patient leave little opportunity for a final pious thought, a witty or wise last word or a beatific smile – all of which, by tradition and temperament, are options I find attractive. It would be nice to live up to them, but embarrassing to fail, so perhaps the less said now the better.

It is interesting to see how easily my first response borders on flippancy. Is that merely a defence mechanism against contemplating the unacceptable – my own end? I have contemplated it before. There are, of course, the mini-deaths: the moments of utter shame when I wanted the floor to open up and swallow me – anything rather than face the embarrassment of continued existence. Attempting to sing a newly written song, unaccompanied, as a floor singer in a folk club – forgetting the words, let alone the 'tune', half-way through – losing the audience and my own vulnerable self-respect, and desperately wanting to die or at least vanish from the face of the earth; that was a form of death, real enough in its way. It was just that the stakes were less, the considerations fewer, at the time, even if others could ever intrude into the self-contained, introverted world of that particular teenager struggling to accommodate what was obviously a ferocious ambition locked in a desperately shy frame.

There was, and is, a chronic unease: my grandfather died at the age of fifty as did my mother, for different reasons in each case, but such coincidences colour one's thoughts – more magical thinking. How much time do I have? The numbers are irrelevant and over the years have seemed less important, but as I approach the fateful age for myself, there is a certain ironic nagging that recurs, only to be dismissed.

More fateful are two distinct events. I had made the decision, or felt that it had been made somewhere within me, to become a rabbi and, having completed my medical degree and house jobs for registration, prepared myself for Rabbinic college by studying Hebrew for six months in Jerusalem. My parents were anxious about my going; things looked particularly threatening in the Middle East that year. It amused me (who believes parents' anxieties anyway!) that we had to stop over for a night in Athens on the way, because we landed in the middle of a revolution. That one they had not anticipated! Surely their little son was perfectly safe.

Two months later in Jerusalem, in June 1967, things suddenly spiralled towards a major confrontation between Israel and Egypt and hence the rest of Israel's neighbours. Everyone knew war was coming and no one had any ideas about the outcome. Solidarity with the Jewish people demanded that I stay. But I had sufficient distaste for the notion of a war that I toyed with the idea of offering my medical services, severely limited as they were, to some 'neutral' medical agency so that I could serve 'both sides'. In the event I volunteered for work at Hadassah hospital and ultimately sat out the Six-Day War doing episiotomy repairs in the delivery room. But all of this was theoretical and mock heroic in the days before the war. What made it suddenly real was the stencilled letter from Her Majesty's Government to the effect that 'in the event of hostilities breaking out Her Majesty's Government could not take responsibility for the safety of its citizens and therefore recommended that they take urgent steps to leave the country'. The later discovery that an identical letter had gone out just before the War of Independence in 1948 (simply substituting the date and country on the standard issue form?) did little to alleviate the chill of feeling utterly abandoned – or rather of recognising that I had made a decision of solidarity with Jewish destiny at this moment, even if it meant my own life. I do not remember it as being a particularly hard decision. Surely it was reinforced by the similar behaviour of all around me and perhaps by a certain inertia, a desire not to 'lose face'? But I felt in no way forced. Nor did the prospect of my own death mean that much. My letters home at the time were all vaguely reassuring. I had no other ties or responsibilities. The theologian Ignaz Maybaum, writing about the 'Binding of Isaac' in Genesis 22, accepts the Rabbinic view that Isaac went willingly to his possible death as a sacrifice to God, for what have young people to offer other than their zeal and willingness for self-sacrifice? Only maturity brings the responsibilities that make life itself seem the greater challenge than death.

In the event Israel was overwhelmingly victorious in an absurdly short space of time. The deaths that took place hardly touched me; they were newsreel shots – this despite helping with the casualties flooding the hospital corridors, 'theirs' rather than 'ours' (another terrible failure of imagination). If anything the war, which had startling and, in retrospect, disturbing effects upon the whole Jewish psyche, affected me less than those back home. For once I was there on the spot, not absent and thus guilty by default, and I value that detachment. But even that contemplation of death did little to affect my own inner sense of security. If anything, the war reinforced the absurd belief in my own invulnerability that keeps death comfortably and firmly at bay.

It took another event to shatter that security and it is recent enough still to have consequences and distress. The tale is simply told. Following the death of my father, my sister and I inherited a property which we sold for a tidy sum. We invested the money in increasing amounts in a business that went bust. In that lunatic innocence and greed of the gambler, we invested again with the same entrepreneur. It did not help to be advised later that the whole enterprise was 'dodgy' from the start. What was distressing was the greed and incompetence of a variety of 'professionals' whom we had to mobilise at various stages to deal with the business. But these are only details, though I still feel a sense of anger and hopelessness about the matter from time to time. What is relevant here was the shock to my system for the period of a couple of years as I watched these vast sums of money disappearing, whilst I remained under constant pressure, for months at a time, to make decisions, sometimes daily, in a situation over which I had absolutely no control. What seemed like an inevitable slide into bankruptcy or worse shattered that sense of my own invulnerability. Lillian Hellman writes of 'middle-class security' as a 'faith' which helped her through her own financial disasters, but for a time for me that, too, was gone.

Even the decision at some point to fight back, which came after an ultimatum from the entrepreneur, did little to alleviate the inner fears, the waking up with anxiety attacks in the early hours of the morning, endless scenarios of disaster playing through my mind, being unreachable by others at certain times – all ironically accompanying a major period of success in my public life, marked by the appearance of a major prayer book and the imminent appointment as Principal of a Rabbinic Seminary. It was operating in that 'real world', and feeling a responsibility to live up to the values with which I had so carefully imbued the prayer book, that helped pull me through the worst. I took a bitter symbolic satisfaction in typing the passages for a new religious anthology on the back of notepaper printed up for our disastrous 'business'. I translated the lessons of this experience into potential sermons, and got on with life with all the resources I could muster.

But in those darker moments thoughts of death intruded. Suppose the worst came to the worst, that we went financially bust. In the circumstance (and this is part of the tunnel view of depression), I would have to give up my job, as I would become a source of embarrassment to the movement that employed me in such a prominent position. Unable to maintain my family we would have to sell our house, perhaps move abroad, etc. etc. The possibility of death as a way out of all these problems was suddenly very comforting; whatever happened, there was at least one solution.

I do not think that even at the lowest moments it was ever a real or likely option, not because of any great religious concern, but rather because of a sort of saving irony that mocked this self-dramatisation – it was only money, and life had other more important elements, not least my wife and children. Perhaps there was also vague resentment that such scoundrels would have the final say and, ultimately, a sense of trust in God still to sort things out in His terms, even if not in the comfortable and conventional ones I might want. It was faith rather than any specific religious teaching that made the difference.

The Jewish Way of Death

If I turn to 'Jewish teachings' about death, it is hard to know what to record or emphasise. This life is neither the beginning nor end of the existence of the soul – that is, some essence of identity, a personal 'me'. The Hebrew Bible says little about an 'afterlife' but it knows a lot of terms for the location of the dead, some related to the earth and burial (*kever*, the grave, *afar*, the dust), others to the underworld (*sheol*; *bor*, *shahat*, the 'pit', a place of gloom and silence) which seem to be part of the inherited tradition of Near Eastern religion. A 'good' death leaves the deceased buried with his or her ancestors; conversely, failure to bury the dead, even the corpse of a murderer, is a scandal and disgrace.

The Hebrew Bible records three 'suicides', including Samson's martyrdom and Saul's death to avoid capture by the enemy. The third, told in a most laconic style, is the death of Ahitophel. Having advised Absolom in his revolt against David, Ahitophel is the first to realise that the rebellion will not succeed and that he will be disgraced and destroyed when David is restored. 'He saddled his ass, and arose, and got him home, unto his city, and set his house in order, and strangled himself; and he died, and was buried in the sepulchre of his father' (2 Samuel 17:23). He is accorded surprising dignity and respect for his end.

Rabbinic Judaism, in its customary way, is both less and more generous. Clearly, the topic must be studied and ruled upon, but it is only in relatively late Rabbinic texts that suicide is condemned as a sin that is an attack upon the life that God has given us.

However, when there is present a situation of duress (when one is forced to murder another to avoid committing public idolatry, for example), one may take one's own life rather than commit the greater sin. Similarly martyrdom, so as to sanctify the name of God, was considered permissible, such as the mass suicide that took place at Masada under the Roman siege, or later in Jewish communities under attack in Christian Europe during the Middle Ages. But even in private situations, the rabbis recognised a distinction between someone who took their own life with premeditation, having announced the deed beforehand, and someone found dead, where suicide might be presumed, yet no evidence of deliberate intent was available. In the latter case it was to be assumed that the death was not intentional, or that their mind was temporarily deranged and they could not be held responsible for the actions. In the past a known suicide would have been buried in a special part of the cemetery, but increasingly today the presumption is made that the act was committed whilst the deceased was of unsound mind or afterwards had regretted taking their action but were by then powerless to stop the process.

What sort of 'afterlife' there might be is not spelled out in the Hebrew Bible. Scholars argue whether the absence of such information implies there is no developed concept or merely that it was so taken for granted that it need not be discussed in any detail. Two biblical figures were 'taken' straight to heaven (Enoch and Elijah) which was clearly seen as a special grace. If the Hebrew Bible knows of some place with God at the end of this life, then the most moving expression of it (though it depends on how you translate and interpret the passage) is the statement in Psalm 73:23–4:

> Yet I am always with You.
> You have grasped me by the hand.
> You will guide me with Your counsel,
> and afterwards receive me in glory.

Rabbinic Judaism makes a few half-hearted attempts to 'prove' an 'afterlife' from Scripture, but the proofs are based on forced readings of verbal tenses. For example Moses 'will' sing a song, after his own death, and ignore more obvious options. But, as usual in Rabbinic thinking, no consistently argued position is given as *the* view, and different opinions are scattered throughout the literature.

The point to make, of course, as Jewish apologists have frequently done, is that Judaism is a 'this-worldly' religion, as opposed to the 'other worldliness' of Christianity. Neither of these two perceptions quite stands up to examination (both religions are big enough to contain all sorts of possible views), but certainly Judaism invests a lot in our 'this-worldly' responsibilities and has to wrestle constantly with the unfairness of life. An 'afterlife' that will remove all inequities and resolve all problems is clearly available in Jewish theology, but is not turned to in the first instance. If suffering comes, the rabbis argue, examine your deeds and seek the failure within yourself. If no such sins can be found, then there is a concept of 'sufferings of love', things imposed upon the righteous by God either as a way of testing them or because of some higher purpose. Rather than the simple view of reward and punishment, which Judaism tends to view as more applicable to the collectivity of Israel rather than the individual, there is a concept that 'the reward of sin is sin, and the reward of good deeds is the opportunity to do further good deeds'; we create our own fate in this world.

Death is inevitable – everyone dies – but it may come sooner than the end of one's life span as a result of sin, though ample opportunity is offered to 'return', that is, away from wrong-doing and back to God. Death itself has an atoning power even for the greatest sinner. The rabbis assumed that the dead must go through some sort of after-death evaluation of their lives for a limited period, including punishment where appropriate, but that after this period, a maximum of one year, the pure soul returns to God.

Thus mourning for one's parents, by reciting the Kaddish prayer daily, is to cease after eleven months; to continue further might imply that they were such great sinners that they had not yet left purgatory. In fact, the rabbis were astonishingly generous in this matter and reckoned that only four biblical characters were so evil that they had no share of the world to come, and even went on to make allowance for some of these. Again, at the risk of appearing flippant, if an 'afterlife' is an important concern for someone's individual religious needs, Judaism is a comforting faith.

The paradox of the relation between death and life is exquisitely expressed in certain Rabbinic statements from the Sayings of the Fathers (4:21–2):

Rabbi Jacob says: 'This world is like a corridor to the world to come. Prepare yourself in the corridor so that you may enter the inner chamber.' He used to say: 'One hour of repentance and good deeds in this world is better than all the life of the world to come, and one hour of calmness of spirit in the world to come is better than all the life of this world.'

Perhaps more important than theories about the nature of death and its consequences are the degree to which the reality of death is infused into one's daily religious life and how far the religion itself prepares the individual for that reality. The community shares with the individual the mourning of his or her own deceased. For the daily and subsequently annual memorial prayer to be recited, a *minyan* (a quorum of ten adult males) is required, at least

71

in orthodox circles, thus the death is 'shared' with the community. The presence of the mourner means that we all have this constant reminder of death before us, something that might have been taken for granted in the past but seems problematic in our contemporary society.

The rabbis saw sleep as a sixtieth part of death, so that we have to acknowledge each morning that with our waking the soul has actually been restored to us. Hence one of the first prayers to be recited in the daily morning service:

My God, the soul You have given me is pure, for You created it, You formed it and You made it live within me. You watch over it within me, but one day You will take it from me to everlasting life. My God and God of my ancestors, as long as the soul is within me, I will declare that You are the master of all deeds, the ruler of all creatures, and the Lord of every soul. Blessed are You, Lord, who restores souls to dead bodies.

The theologian and philosopher Franz Rosenzweig has drawn attention to the way that the Day of Atonement (Yom Kippur), on which the worshippers traditionally wear white garments that will ultimately serve as their shrouds, dramatises for each person their own death. For that one day a year when we fast for twenty-five hours and are thus cut off from many of the normal biological functions of life, we are 'as if' dead, and can thus view our lives with the dispassionate detachment of the grave. To experience that 'mini-death' can be a very helpful preparation for contemplating and confronting that real death to come. 'Plan for this world as if you were to live forever; plan for the world to come as if you were to die tomorrow' (Solomon Ibn Gabirol).

This pragmatism in the face of death is ultimately comforting precisely because it is singularly unsentimental. Again one of the Sayings of the Fathers, attributed to Rabbi Elazar Hakappar, gives a powerful summary of the parameters of life (4:29):

Without your consent you were born, and without your consent you live, and without your consent you die, and without your consent you will have to give an account and a reckoning before the King above the kings of kings, The Holy One, blessed be He.

Another saying attributed to Rabbi Akiba, who himself suffered a martyr's death at the hands of the Romans, is surprisingly cheerful, not only in its general tone, but in its final promise (Sayings of the Fathers, 3:20):

He used to say, 'Everything is given on pledge, and a net is spread for all the living. The shop is open, and the shopkeeper gives credit, and the account is open and the hand writes, and whoever wishes to borrow may come and borrow. But the collectors go round every day, and exact payment from people with their consent or without it, and their claims are justified, and the judgement is a judgement of truth. Yet everything is prepared for the feast!'

The Death of Another

Except for the two occasions mentioned previously, I have rarely had to think about my own death in quite such challenging ways. It is the death of others, or their impending death, that has most often broken through my defences. It was that awareness that helped in the selection of readings and the formulation of prayers for a Funeral Prayer Book I co-edited for the Reform Synagogues of Great Britain. Funerals are for the survivors as much as for the deceased. The materials that are there to be studied or prayed may help to give comfort and consolation to those most directly affected, but they also enable all who are present to gain some perspective upon their own mortality.

I suppose that I have a professional interest in the advancing of that information. One of the prices we have paid in gaining our secular world is the breakdown of the ritualised 'rites of passage' of our tradition. The stages of birth, barmitzvah, marriage, parenthood, ageing and death were marked by Jewish tradition, so that such transitions were given their collective and individual worth. Perhaps it is only romantic to imagine that things were clearer in the past, but certainly there were advantages to having yardsticks or points of identification as we went through the bewildering course of our lives. When such yardsticks are absent, or only present in a truncated or crude form (witness the vulgarity of the average barmitzvah celebration), then for all that is gained in freedom, something is also lost in understanding and interpreting the changes in our lives. Perhaps this matters less in earlier stages, but in the crisis that is often experienced once we pass middle age or with retirement, and certainly when we are gradually confronted with our own ultimate death, there are insights and supports offered by religion that can no longer be called upon. We lack even a common language of faith with which to begin a conversation with each other. Only that which may be conveyed 'in advance' can be of help.

This thought was triggered by memories of two particular deaths. The first was of a woman whom I hardly knew. She was that typically anonymous creature, a patient in a hospital ward, dying of cancer and trying desperately to speak with her physicians about letting her die. At the time I was a houseman, totally unprepared by my training or life experience to talk with her. She spoke insistently about 'doing it'. What that 'it' was remained undeclared, because no language of discourse was available. One did not talk about asking for death in a British hospital over twenty years ago. There was no hospice movement, no counselling skills, no way for me to step outside my medical role and even attempt to talk about what she really wanted. It was clear to the registrar what was wanted and needed. He made up the prescription for a painkilling concoction that, with increasing doses, would remove her pain for ever. But for me the personal sense of grotesque inadequacy and hopelessness was deeply disturbing. What if she might still magically recover? How could one take such a risk? And yet how could one not respond to the pain and her desperate mute attempt to ask us to end it for her? It was out of my hands at the time, but the frustration and anger remained, to surface on a later occasion when I had less excuse to evade the issue.

As a student rabbi I had to work part-time with a congregation, a task restricted mostly to conducting religious services and teaching. I was rarely involved in pastoral work, and it was some time after I had left the congregation when a member asked me to visit his wife who was dying of cancer in hospital.

I went with reluctance and anxiety, still untrained in such matters and generally uncomfortable with such visits. So we talked banalities; rather, I did most of the talking, filling every silence as quickly as possible, desperately avoiding the reality of her illness and possible death. At the end of half an hour I left, relieved to have 'done my duty', but aware that I had not really been of use. A few days later, her husband phoned to ask me to visit her again. She was angry with me, he said, without explaining why. Perhaps, again, she could not express the things most on her mind, and I had done nothing to help her. I hardly remember the conversation, and I do not know how far it was of value to her. I know that it enabled me to break through my own reserve and it seemed to have offered her the opportunity to speak that she so desperately needed.

What remains above all, for me, is her seriousness. We are so unprepared for seriousness; we function on habit, politeness, superficialities and second-hand information and opinions. It is a safe way of living, but no use for the seriousness of dying. We have no vocabulary of belief we can share unless we belong to a particular religious community that is willing to be honest about such matters.

There are now, of course, as well as the remarkable hospice movement, secular 'communities' that are willing to confront the questions of our life and death. My next-door neighbour of some years ago was a remarkable woman who had dedicated her life to the service of socialism. She had been an activist and campaigner for many causes and was a person of great integrity and devotion to duty. But one day she confided that she felt she had now achieved all that she could. Her children were grown up, her financial situation was secure, she felt that she had nothing more to fight for, having done her duty, and she was really waiting to die. But two months later she was revived by a new cause she had taken up. It had really brought her back to life she told me, quite unaware of the irony of her remarks. For the cause was 'Exit', now renamed as an organisation concerned with voluntary euthanasia.

At the time it was campaigning to make information available to the public on how to take one's life when circumstances made it necessary. Her enthusiasm was infectious, her arguments impeccable, her anger at the attempts to prevent the dissemination of information on suicide (familiar from her other campaigns) remained quite legitimate. I do not know if she had come to terms with her own death, or was still challenging death to come to terms with her. But here was a community, secular and religious (a valued Rabbinic colleague was a member), offering mutual support to its members in the face of the unthinkable, their own necessary death.

Euthanasia, itself, is unacceptable to traditional Judaism. Life is sacred and must be preserved at all costs. Nothing should be done, according to Jewish law, to hasten the death of someone, even rearranging the furniture in the room if that might have such an effect. But one *is* allowed to pray for the death of someone who is dying and in severe distress. Indeed to do so may even amount to a positive command. To interfere directly would be tantamount to murder; to pray for an end of suffering is to surrender one's desires into the hands of God and trust in God's mercy.

The End of the Matter, All Having Been Heard

So I have at times prayed for the death of another, as I hope others will pray for my death when the time comes, if the suffering is too great to bear. Jewish tradition speaks of a sweet release given to the righteous and the 'kiss of death' delivered by God. Moses had such a death, according to one Rabbinic view, though the ancient exposition of the Scriptures, the Midrash, also records his long arguments with God to allow him to live on and not to die. King David similarly fought the angel of death, and only died when his attention was diverted through a trick.

Should we look for resignation or a struggle to the end? I remember Lily Pincus, a remarkable woman who turned her own life difficulties and tragedies into things of enormous value for others.

When her husband died she explored her own bereavement and wrote on it. In her old age she studied the ageing process and taught ways that people could still gain value from their lives. When she learned that she was soon to die, she refused treatment that she knew would be more distressing than the natural end. Her publisher, perhaps half jesting, asked her to write about the process of dying and she agreed but added, with the seriousness that was hers alone, that it was likely to be a rather short book. She lived to see the proofs.

But that is the way to go. Like another remarkable woman, Anneliese Debray, an old friend who turned a pious Catholic Women's conference centre in Germany into a pioneering place for the work of post-war reconciliation between Germans and the nations they had harmed, and particularly between German Christians and Jews. After her retirement she created new tasks for herself, but died suddenly and totally unexpectedly of a heart attack on a railway station platform about to board a train on her way to yet another meeting. She died in harness.

Such an end was the one envisaged for Moses by the theological writer Werner Pelz. Moses dies on the verge of entering the promised land, and this is seen as a great tragedy and the result of some sin he had committed. But Pelz recognised another truth. Had Moses entered the land with the Israelites he would have had to live with

78

the bureaucracy, the inefficiency, the mundane realities and banalities of the new settlement. To die with a vision still before him, a task to achieve, a hope yet to be fulfilled, 'with eye undimmed and his natural force unabated', that was not a curse but a blessing. I would like such an end for myself, but nothing is guaranteed. So I take comfort from the following strange Hasidic parable:

The souls descended from the realms of heaven to earth on a long ladder. Then it was taken away. Now up there they are calling home the souls. Some do not budge from the spot, for how can one get to heaven without a ladder? Others leap and fall and leap again and give up. But there are those who know very well that they cannot achieve it, but try and try, over and over again, until God catches hold of them and pulls them up.

QUITE FRIENDLY
UP TO DEATH

The Revd Canon John A. White,
St George's Chapel, Windsor Castle

*Though born in the Midlands, John White spent his
formative years in the north of England. After attending
Batley Grammar School he had a period in the Civil
Service and school-teaching before reading history and
theology at Hull University prior to ordination training
at the College of the Resurrection, Mirfield. A curacy in
Leeds led to work at the University Chaplaincy after which
he went to teach theology on the newly founded North West
(later Northern) Ordination Course then seen as a major
'experiment' in part-time ministerial training. After nine
years he was appointed to a canonry at St George's Chapel,
Windsor Castle which, alongside his other responsibilities, gives him the opportunity, at St George's House
Conference Centre, to work with both in-service training
of the clergy and 'secular' consultations, especially in the
field of education.*

*Out there, we've walked quite friendly up to Death;
Sat down and eaten with him, cool and bland, –*
Wilfred Owen, 'The Next War'

My parents' only other child, my sister, died at the
age of seven from diphtheria, seven years before I was
born. This fact, accompanied by my mother's recurrent

ill health, in part the result of a misplaced sense of guilt associated with Jean Mary's failure to recover from what was still, in the thirties, often a fatal illness, made me, from an early age, deeply conscious of mortality. Unlike many of my schoolfriends, who were raised in a childhood atmosphere no longer regularly perfumed by the lilies of the valley clutched in some dead sibling's cold clasp, I lived closely alongside the idea of death. Just as Wilfred Owen's doomed soldiers accept death as a companion, whistling while he shaved them with his scythe, I acquired some sense of control over this domestic but mysterious finality. Perhaps it is these early influences which make me today an enthusiast for musical settings of the Requiem Mass. Certainly it was the attempt to come to terms with death which gave rise to some of my earliest quarrels with the Christian orthodoxy of my Sunday School teachers.

My elderly father had himself 'walked quite friendly up to Death' when he was one amongst those trench dwellers recorded by Owen in the poetry which had the pity of war as its subject. In demonstration of his familiarity with death my mother told the story of his standing asleep during the worst air raids of the Second World War, whilst waiting for a lull in which he might organise the local group of fire fighters. This did not surprise me, for my father was a deeply self-possessed man who rarely showed signs of anger and proved impossible to provoke. He was not impressed by death and certainly had no fear of it. However, this dearly loved father was not in the strictest sense of the word a Christian. From his youth he had professed the Unitarian faith, having shared his teenage years with many of those Birmingham entrepreneurs who belonged to Hurst Street Chapel. It became clear to me in later life, when I was studying theology, that his objection to the doctrine of the Divinity of Christ was unequivocal. He disliked all dogma and the moralising that takes no account of human nature. So whilst he supported me with encouragement and finance so that I might be ordained to the Christian priesthood, he did not for one moment accept the basic tenets of the Christian Creed. Yet from earliest memory I cannot recall ever accepting that he would after death go to Hell for his heterodoxy.

My mother had clear Christian conviction, so clear that she could not remove the fearful sense that God would judge her and find her wanting. Although she clutched at every straw which might bring her relief from the burden of guilt, she could never truly rid her mind of the awful warnings that had been part of her early upbringing. She was not a rigorist in her ethical view of others; in fact she was generous to a fault in refusing to judge moral failures. I remember as a small child at the close of the war being gently reprimanded for including Hitler's name in my battle games as such a personalisation of evil seemed to her to be unchristian. But despite her natural inclination to follow Madame de Staël, '*Tout comprendre rend très indulgent*,' she could not find the conviction that God would be as generous to her as he would be to anyone else. For my mother the fear was that 'behind a frowning providence' he hid a frowning face! That traditional deterrent of Christian theology, namely the Last Judgement, only added distress to her already unhappy spirit. Recognising this compelled me to question whether there could be any basis for such a doctrine. If eternal punishment was to be understood as some heavenly arsenal compelling mortals towards the good life for fear the armoury would be launched against them, whilst in fact there existed no plan for its eventual use, then in my mother's case the threat had not worked. Her life had been far from fulfilled, rather it had been marred by the oppressive combination of guilt and judgement. If, however, eternal punishment was more than a mere threat and was to be poured out on the unrepentant sinner, then it appeared to me that my mother's sense of compassion exceeded that attributed to the loving God. For she could never have assented to St Augustine's cold but biting logic that a joy of heaven is to watch the will of God perfected in the sufferings of the damned in hell.

Despite the conviction of many modern-day keepers of the necropolis (we ministers of religion who commit the bodies of unknown deceased in crematorium and cemetery), that our function is to bring comfort to the bereaved, the developed orthodoxy we represent has little absolute comfort to propose. For since the Middle Ages the dominant thought concerning the afterlife has been that of judgement. In the Catholic tradition punishment has been shared between Purgatory and Hell. In the Reformed tradition, eschewing unbiblical doctrines of purgation, the options have been more stark. That child of the parsonage, Charlotte Brontë, caught the mood of the moment when she included the conversation between young Jane Eyre and the Rev. Mr Brocklehurst of Lowood School:

'No sight so sad as that of a naughty child,' he began, 'especially a naughty little girl. Do you know where the wicked go after death?'

'They go to hell,' was my ready and orthodox answer.

'And what is hell? Can you tell me that?'

'A pit full of fire.'

'And should you like to fall into that pit, and be burning there for ever?'

'No, sir.'

'What must you do to avoid it?'

I deliberated a moment; my answer, when it did

come, was objectionable: 'I must keep in good health, and not die.'

'How can you keep in good health? Children younger than you die daily. I buried a little child of five years old only a day or two since, – a good little child, whose soul is now in heaven. It is to be feared the same could not be said of you were you to be called hence.'

Even though Mr Brocklehurst is a minister of the Reformed tradition his words carry the same burden as those of the 'Dies Irae' of the Latin Mass. They both represent what became the dominant mood of late medieval Christianity, that is the need to escape the damnation of Hell or mitigate the agonies of Purgatory. The confidence shown in the early Christian communities, when the day of death was called the 'heavenly birthday' and thus was to be remembered by an annual party, disappeared under a pall of guilt and condemnation. The fourth-century rustic epitaph from Asia Minor, recalled by Dom Gregory Dix in *The Shape of the Liturgy* (Dacre Press, 1945), 'Here sleeps the blessed Chione, who has found Jerusalem for she prayed much,' seems a religion away from the representations of maggot-filled decomposing corpses that sealed many late medieval tombs.

Although it was unplanned, around the age of forty I suddenly realised that I had arrived at a watershed in life. This became apparent in two changes of attitude. The first was that until this point, life was still an open possibility for which I was preparing, and from this point clearly it had to be lived! The second was a radical change in my attitude to the authority of religion in my living. For most, if not all, of my remembered past religion had set the standard towards which I was to aspire and against which I always proved to have given short measure. Then, suddenly, I realised that religion had to prove itself as being useful in the interpretation of the life which I lived. For religion needed to justify itself to me if I was to continue in any way to see it as a legitimate means to my self-development and personal happiness. My maxim became: religion must be about life, not life about religion. I found that I could accommodate this change of viewpoint without too much upheaval to my scrupulous moral sense (not the same as practice, of course!) because I had come at the same time to recognise religion as a human product, a product which emerged in response to a human recognition of divinity. God was clearly greater than religion and could in no way be contained by its important but fragmentary expressions.

The result of this sea-change was that I became more interested in questions of the significance of the present life than in speculations about the next. Perhaps it was a spiritualising of my maternal grandmother's oft repeated view that you must 'take care of the pennies and the pounds will look after themselves'. I was, however, left in some confusion, as I could not see how in any Christian understanding of the nature of God and our human destiny this life could have real significance. For if God is beyond change and his will is ultimately always fulfilled, and if our 'naughty' world is simply a stage on which this reality is worked out in a great drama of creation, then what I say and do and think, what I destroy or create, whatever of my potential I realise or fail to realise, what loves I make or break, what truths I discover or lies I perpetrate, all these seem to have no eternal consequence, by which I mean that finally they have nothing to do with the Creative Reality which lies at the centre of all that is. I have a vested interest in keeping some adherence to traditional Christianity but I was also endowed by nature with a stronger urge to pursue what appears to be true, and thus there seemed to be emerging an irreconcilable tension between the religion of my cultural roots and my need to discover if this life in fact forms the basis of what is real. I was loath to renounce my Christian allegiance because I recognised that much of what I most valued in my understanding of both the immanence and transcendence of the Divine came from this background. Moreover I had no wish to remove myself from the company of those who had, through the centuries, shared a common belief in human dignity and Divine compassion inspired by the life and teaching of Jesus of Nazareth.

Whilst I was becalmed in this sea of emotional and intellectual uncertainty I came upon the writings of Charles Péguy. It was essentially an act of serendipity which introduced me to this French poet and thinker who died whilst leading his men against the first German advance into France in 1914. I had bought his biography in a sale of publishers' overstock and was inspired to read it having come across a quotation of his in a book by Alan Ecclestone. It was in this biography that I found the words which formed the necessary catalyst to enable the reaction to occur between my inherited tradition and my own experience-based insight:

Il dépend de nous chrétiennes,
Que l'eternel ne manque point de temporel,
(Singulier renversement)
... Que Dieu ne manque point de sa création.

It depends on us Christians,
That the eternal does not lack the temporal,
(Strange reversal)
... That God does not lack his creation.
Charles Péguy, *Le Porche du Mystère de la Deuxième*
Vertu

At the heart of the Christian religion is a belief that the Creator is incarnate within his creation. This faith is expressed through the complex doctrines of Christology, many of which seem to lack the force today that they once held some seventeen hundred years ago. Belief in incarnation is not wholly unique to the Christian religion, nevertheless it is that religion's particular contribution to the most difficult of faith patterns, namely belief in One God. This incarnational insight has an appeal for me, which is reinforced by Péguy's assertion about the role of the Christian in making the temporal available for incorporation in the eternal, that is to say in the being of God. Often incarnation is seen as a one-way activity, that of God entering our human condition, but there is a strain within the Christian tradition which speaks of humanity being 'divinised' through this process, which seems to be the natural and necessary consequence. Since I recognised that religion is a human product I have also recognised that the language of religion is a strange alchemy of the poetic, the mythical, the philosophical and occasionally the historical. It is impossible to unpick any one strand without destroying the fabric. But it is also improper to pretend that the cloth is made of a single type of thread. We can do no more than struggle for meaning but we must struggle so that we have some small purchase on the reality of which we are a part and which we may significantly help to create.

Affirming the eternal importance of this life as the continuous expression of the incarnation of God affects the way I now look at death. We are involved in endless opportunities for creativity, some of which we take and some of which we reject. The origin of creativity is what we choose to call love. The true test of love is if it proves creative, both for the lover and the beloved.

My Christian tradition is clear in its affirmation of the primacy of love and has even been bold enough to say that God is Love. So it is that we encourage love as the basis of our common life and affirm it as central to marriage, family and friendship. The more we commit ourselves to such love, the more stark and cruel the separation of death appears. For love, as the basis of our common humanity, affirms its very corporateness. We need one another in order to find ourselves. As John Donne said, 'No Man is an ilande, intire of it selfe' thus pointing to the fact that we only enter the terrifying state of an isolated individual at the moment when we die. This reality was brought closely to my attention by a one-time student of mine who went to use her skills in physiotherapy and pastoral care at a hospice. After four years she was asked to reflect on her work at a meeting with members of the staff. She said that dying was clearly a very lonely experience and this brought the immediate response that if this were the case more people should be at the bedside of those *in extremis*. She then attempted to point out that death was irretrievably a lonely experience for it can only be accomplished alone. If, therefore, we are to find our human fulfilment, if love is the source of creativity and we are mysteriously part of the eternal love, then we must be restored to some corporateness, to some mutuality, if we are not to be lost for ever to the creative process.

It is this nagging thought which prevents me from accepting with calm resignation my father's view that there is, for us human beings, nothing which we may call eternal life. However, I cannot accept as adequate interpretations of death many of the views which have been held in the long history of the faith which I share. I believe that death itself is a part of the creative pattern of the world. It was around a long time before *Homo sapiens* arrived on the planet and I expect it to be there long after our race has disappeared. This being the case death is not, as St Paul, following one particular Scriptural view, thought it, a punishment for sin. We were never intended to live for ever. Neither do I hold that death serves as a point of judgement when our faith and works are tested. I have been too much distressed by the anxiety of Christian parents, who, losing a child in the middle of adolescent atheism, add to their grief a fear for that child's eternal salvation. Nor can I begin to visualise a heaven where our 'resurrected' bodies go to live for ever. The main characteristic of being human is that we change and that we are constantly in process of becoming something different. Our bodies are not susceptible to an eternal state of arrest and if they were, at what point in life would we be so preserved? I have often heard the complaint that such questionings are the product of a lack of true faith, but it seems to me an insult to our human dignity to suggest that we cannot tease out some of the elements of absurdity which are caught, like slubs, in the fabric of our tradition of faith.

I do believe that our human life has a purpose and that we are capable of being genuinely creative. I see this present ever-changing life as integral to any proper understanding of eternal life, that is the life of the very being of God. The logical consequence of accepting a theology which sees God as incarnate, thus making himself known by sharing in the created order and especially in human life, is that we accept that our human life also finds its fulfilment in its participation in the life of God. Clearly we are differentiated by our separate existences in separate bodies. Those bodies, which include our minds, ultimately die as complex integrated organisms and we lose our individual self-consciousness. However, at our death we leave our creative imprint on the very nature of God and, as a seal finds its purpose in the impression made on the wax, so we find our final purpose in the impression we make as our part in God's continuing creativity and self-realisation.

It interests me to see, in the New Testament, amongst the complex accounts and interpretations of the resurrected Jesus, that there is a view which holds that the risen Lord continues to live in the life of the community of believers who follow his teaching and example. This view comes from the knowledge that for any change to occur as a result of the life of Jesus in the future, others living in different times and places have to embody what they have learned from him in their own lives. St Teresa of Avila encapsulated this in her often quoted, but perhaps rarely assimilated, proposition: 'Christ has no body now on earth but yours, no hands but yours, no feet but yours. Yours are the eyes through which must look out Christ's compassion on the world. Yours are the feet with which he is to go about doing good. Yours are the hands with which he is to bless us now.'

I am left, therefore, with two views to hold together in paradox. The first is the affirmation that this life is the place where God is actively creative and thus realises his loving purposes. It is, therefore, in this life that we make our contribution to the pattern of history, leaving behind us, after death, an indelible, if unhailed, imprint. The second is that God's relationship to his world is such that we also leave some impression upon his eternal nature simply by having been. In this way we may be said to have a dimension to our self-hood which is beyond but incorporating the temporal. Thus, as we are ourselves creative and as we encourage the world around us to be creative we bring what is temporal into the sphere of what is eternal. The two faces of this coinage of our being are held together through the experience of love. Love is used here to express more than emotional attachment, though it in no way excludes the passions. It is that unity between us which transcends the passing of time and even the separation of death. It is the creative energy which always seeks, phoenix-like, to make new life from the ashes of the old.

If I am to continue to grow in my understanding and awareness then I must recognise the essential provisionality of all my thinking and that in my generation there are limits beyond which I cannot go for lack of available knowledge. However, at this point in my pilgrimage I feel able to say that death is not the gateway to a new future but part of *'la même route droite'* (to use a phrase of Péguy), that highly privileged journey which we share in the continuing creative expression of the love of God.

> *The stone fidelity*
> *They hardly meant has come to be*
> *Their final blazon, and to prove*
> *Our almost-instinct almost true:*
> *What will survive of us is love.*
> Philip Larkin, 'An Arundel Tomb'

THE CONCEPT OF DEATH IN SIKHISM

Professor Harmindar Singh

Harmindar Singh is well known in the British Sikh community as an expert on the Sikh religion, and is secretary of the Sikh Divine Fellowship. After gaining a degree in English he became a professor in India where he still spends time each year. He is deeply committed to the work of inter-faith dialogue and is Vice-chairman of the World Conference on Religion for Peace (UK branch). He is also on the executive of the World Congress of Faiths, appears on television and is in demand as a lecturer and speaker. He is married, and has three adult children and several grandchildren.

> *Birth and death by Divine Ordinance occur;*
> *Under Divine Will beings come and go.*
> (Guru Granth Sahib, p. 472)

> *It is He [God] who sends beings into the world,*
> *And it is He who calls them back.'*
> (ibid. p. 1239)

The above two quotations from the Sikh Scripture, Guru Granth Sahib, summarise the Sikh belief about the natural phenomenon of birth and death. One being the beginning and the other the end of life in this world, both are generally referred to together. Human beings

are born and then ultimately die in accordance with God'
Will. This is a cosmic process of creation and dissolution
operating solely under His command. We, the human
beings, have no say in it:

> All beings by Divine Ordinance arise,
> And by the Ordinance in action engage.
> Some by the Ordinance to death submit;
> Some by the Ordinance in truth are absorbed.
> Saith Nanak: This happens as the Lord wills;
> Nothing in the hand of human beings lies.
>
> (ibid. p. 55)

According to Sikh theology, God created this universe
to please Himself and to enjoy the grand spectacle as a
sort of 'play'. We, the Sikhs, are enjoined to look at
it in the same spirit, including the phenomenon of birth
and death:

> His own play the Lord enacts and views,
> Thus has He raised creation.
>
> (ibid. p. 748)

Since time immemorial, man has been in an earnest
pursuit of finding an answer to the question, what does
'death' mean? Is it the end of personal existence or is there
life after death? Even the fantastic present-day progress
of science and technology, enabling man to soar high into
space, has not helped him in this quest. The mystery of
God's creation, especially of the invisible world of spirit,
can never be unfolded in a science laboratory. God in His
mercy has sent His messengers, the Prophets and Gurus,
at different times and at different places, to reveal and

unveil this mystery to us through Divine Wisdom. It is for us, the believers, to recognise and accept these revelations in good faith.

To fully grasp the concept of death in Sikhism, one must first understand the true nature of man and the purpose of birth and life in this world.

O my mind, thou art a Spark of Divine Light;
    realise thy true Essence.
By realising thy true nature, thou graspest that of
    God,
And thus knowest thou the *mystery of birth and death.*

(ibid. p. 441)

According to Sikh belief and also to other Eastern religions, for example Hinduism, a human being is not just a bundle of bones, flesh, veins and blood for there is a spirit behind this:

Man's body is made of walls of water, pillars
    of air and mud of blood-drops.
In the cage of bones, flesh and blood vessels
    abides the poor bird of life (soul).

(ibid. p. 659)

This spirit, or the soul, is the real self and is part and parcel of the Universal Soul (God). The individual self is Divine in Essence but not in itself the Infinite:

O my body, the Lord put His Divine Spark in thee
    and so thou camest into the world;
Thou camest into the world when the Lord illumined
    thy mind with His Divine Light.

(ibid. p. 921)

94

This soul is immortal, thus it never dies. Only the physical body perishes at the time of death:

Our soul is the image of the Transcendent God.
Neither is this soul old, nor young.
Neither suffers it sorrow, nor is it caught in the
    Yama's noose.
Neither is it wasted away, nor it dies;
Since the beginningless time, it is merged in its self.
(ibid. p. 868)

However, it passes from one life to another until freedom from the shackles of birth and death is attained, when through spiritual evolution it finally merges in the Universal Soul. Just as a man casts away his worn-out clothes and puts on new ones, the soul throws away one physical body to get into another one. Before his human body, man passes through many lives on various planes of existence – plants, animals, birds, etc.:

Numerous trees and plants in our incarnation have
    we gone through;
Numerous are the animal forms in which we were created.
In numerous serpent-forms were we incarnated;
Numerous bird-species on wings did we fly.
(ibid. p. 156)

For several births was I a worm,
For several births an elephant, a fish, a deer;
For several births was I a bird, a serpent,
For several births yoked as a bull, a horse;
After a long period has the human frame come into being,
Seek now union with the Lord of the Universe,
For now is the time.
(ibid. p. 176)

We believe in the transmigration of the soul and its reincarnation. Each birth depends on the actions and spiritual stage of a previous life at the time of death. Our next birth will depend on our present actions and spiritual stage and especially our thoughts and aspirations just before our death:

He who, while dying, thinks of money and dieth worrying
    so,
He is born and reborn as a serpent.
O love, let me not forsake the Name of the Lord.
He who, while dying, thinks of a woman and dieth
    worrying so,
He is recreated again and again as a prostitute;
He who, while dying, thinks of the sons and dieth
    worrying so,
He is born and reborn as a swine.
He who, while dying, thinks of mansions and dieth
    worrying so,
He taketh rebirth as a goblin.
He who dwelleth upon the Lord and dieth reflecting
    thus,
He, sayeth Trilochan, liberated shall be,
The Lord abiding in him.

(ibid. p. 526)

Human birth is thus attained as a result of good deeds, meditation on God and His grace. It is a gift of God, given to us in His mercy and as a part of His blessings. It is also a temple of God as He abides therein. Even the gods covet it because it is only through this vehicle that the ultimate union with the Universal Soul is possible. If one misses the chance, one has again to enter the cycle of births and deaths:

Through the Guru's service and devotion to God,
I acquired this human body.
Even the gods aspire after it.
So meditate on thy Lord through this body.
Dwell thou on God and forget it never.
For the realisation of God is the object of human life.
(ibid. p. 1159)

The ultimate aim and purpose of life is not merely to seek material gains, whether wealth or power. It is gradually and progressively to advance on a spiritual path towards self-realisation and to develop the best in man that is God and then finally merge in Him. It is thus a continuous process of spiritual evolution towards the fulfilment of that final goal of becoming God-like and then remaining perpetually one with Him. Of course, the temporal and secular side of life is not to be ignored but harmoniously blended into a unique and compact pattern by striking a proper balance, after sorting out priorities.

This is certainly not an easy task, as the pleasures of the world distract the mind, which again and again clings to perishable but tempting earthly things. Man is so trapped in these snares that he forgets the inevitability of death. Sikh Gurus have, therefore, laid stress on reminding him of the transitory and fleeting nature of this life and remembering the ultimate end – death:

One eateth and drinketh, maketh merry and sleepeth
    but forgets death,
By abandoning one's Lord, one is wasted away.
O accursed in such a life which stayeth not.
O man, dwell on the Name of thy only God.
That thou goest back to thy Home with Honour and Glory?
(ibid. p. 1254)

Guru Nanak, in his masterpiece known as 'Jupji', which forms part of our daily morning prayer, has mentioned five mystical stages of spiritual ascent, each named as 'Khand' (Realm or Region). These are like five steps of a ladder, leading to the final goal of union with ultimate Truth, God, whose abode is called 'Sachh Khand' (Realm of Eternity or Truth). These five are:

1. 'Dharam Khand'   Realm of Righteousness
2. 'Gian Khand'   Realm of Divine Enlightenment
3. 'Saram Khand'   Realm of Bliss
4. 'Karam Khand'   Realm of Grace
5. 'Sachh Khand'   Realm of Eternal Truth
where God Himself abides

Most Sikh theologians think these just to be spiritual stages of mind but a few believe that each relates to a particular planet in space. After death the soul takes another form of subtle body which goes to the planet corresponding to the spiritual stage of his mind. I have met one great Sikh saint, who has confirmed this on the basis of his own spiritual knowledge and experience. In any case the present explorers of space have not altogether ruled out the possibility of life on other planets.

The individual who happens to attain the final spiritual stage of 'Sachh Khand' when alive, merges in Him after death and thus breaks the cycle of births and deaths. In Sikh parlance he is called 'Jivan Mukta' (Living-Liberated):

One that the Lord's command in mind cherishes,
Is truly to be called 'Jivan Mukta'.
To such a one are joy and sorrow alike;

Ever in joy, never feels he sorrow.
Gold and a clod of earth to him are alike,
As also Amrita [Elixir] and foul-tasting poison.
To him are honour and dishonour alike;
Alike also pauper and prince.
One that such a way practises,
Saith Nanak: a 'Jivan-Mukta' may be called.

(ibid. p. 275)

The servant of God loved his God to the end;
While living, the Lord he served; on leaving the world,
    in mind kept Him.
The Lord's Command with great reverence he obeyed.
The Lord to the servant was gracious;
His life in this world and the next was exalted.
Saith Nanak: Blessed and fulfilled is the servant of God
    unto whom the Lord is revealed thus.

(ibid. p. 1000)

Fear of death has always been a source of constant worry and anxiety to the human race. Young or old, no one wants to die:

All seek to live long enough and no one wants to die.

(ibid. p. 63)

It is common knowledge that the fear which death strikes in one's heart deters one from following the righteous course when that involves risk to life. Anyone in the grip of fear can never advance on the path towards spiritual evolution. One must free oneself from the fear of death to be able to attain a higher standard of moral and spiritual excellence, combined with valour and heroism, being thus bold enough to defend one's religion and freedom of the country.

The last Guru of the Sikhs, Guru Gobind Singh, established the institution of administering 'Amrita' (Elixir or Water of Immortality) to eliminate the fear of death from the hearts of his followers. This Amrita was to make one immortal, in the sense that death was to be nothing but casting away of this physical body, so as to enter through its gateway into the higher realms of spiritual consciousness transcending time, space and causality. Complete surrender demanded at the time of Sikh initiation or Amrita Sanskar (Baptism) metaphorically means death to this world and a new life in the holy spirit of God and Guru. For a 'Jivan Mukta' death is an occasion for rejoicing. The well-known Saint Kabir whose hymns have been incorporated in the Sikh Scripture says:

Death terrifies everyone but it gives joy to me,
For only after death I attain union with the Lord.
(ibid. p. 1364)

Another saint, Ravidas, describes this union with God and identification with His Will while entering into the final stage of 'Sachh Khand' (Realm of Eternal Truth) as follows:

The City Joyful is the name of that city,
Suffering and sorrow abide not there.
Neither is there worry of paying taxes,
Nor fear of punishment for error nor decline.
A beautiful homeland have I found,
Where perpetually reign Peace and Calm, O friend.
Ever-enduring is the regime of my only Lord over there.
There is not a second, nor a third there, but my only Lord.
The city is ever well known,
There the spiritually rich reside.
They disport themselves as they please.

Saith Ravi Das, the cobbler, freed from all bonds
Whoever of that city is denizen, is our friend.

(ibid. p. 345)

This is how a Sikh devotee, through Sikh discipline of meditation on God's name in the ambrosial hours of early morning and with His Grace, becomes a 'Jivan Mukta' and thus conquers death. He attains immortality while he is still in mortal frame. Climbing the five steps of the ladder of spiritual ascent, he finally reaches his Eternal Home, 'Sachh Khand' (Realm of Eternal Truth) and rests peacefully in Divine Bliss. No birth and no death and so no pain. The mystery of death has been revealed to him through Divine Wisdom. He now knows how easy it was to die physically:

Who knows how we shall come to die?
And what manner of death shall we get?
If the Lord is not forgotten,
Then is death easy.
The whole world is of death afraid;
All wish to remain alive,
But he who, by the Guru's Grace, dieth in life,
    he alone knoweth His Will.
Nanak: he who dieth thus, liveth eternally.

(ibid. p. 555)

Reflecting on these teachings I have come to some personal views with which I will conclude. In this modern age of science, technology and materialism, where life is so nerve-straining and hectic, one hardly finds time to think or brood over metaphysical subjects like death. As religious beliefs are at a discount, most people have no idea about the invisible world of spirit and thus of life after death. They only believe in what is perceptible and

101

hence in the philosophy of 'Eat, drink and be merry.' But there are others, though in a minority, who do have a vague idea of the spiritual dimension of this life and the life after death. However, they are also so engrossed in their daily routine of life, that they seldom ponder over the inevitability of death. It is only when some dear one dies that the possibility of their own death occurs to them but this is only momentary and soon passes away. As a Sikh, my own view of death is the same as that put forward by our Divine Gurus and which has been fully expounded in this article. My understanding of the modern scientific and materialistic explanation of death and the interpretation given by other religious prophets has only confirmed my belief in the Sikh tradition and concept of death.

When I was young I hardly ever thought of my own death. However, with the approach of old age and also having gone through some higher spiritual experiences, I have come to think of death almost daily and prepare myself for the inevitable to happen any time. It forms a part of my daily prayer, in which I beg for my death to be sudden and quick, without any suffering to me and my near and dear ones. I feel very strongly that under no circumstances should I be a burden on anyone because of a lingering death due to some prolonged and painful illness. I now remember what my dear mother used to say in her old age: 'My son! I pray and pray daily that I should not die as a result of a prolonged illness, as I do not want to trouble my dear ones, who may have to look after me.' And God did answer her prayers with her sudden and instant death in a road accident. Following in her footsteps, I also pray for a sudden and quick death.

As emphasised by our Gurus, I want to overcome completely the fear of death. However, I am fully aware that it will only be possible when I will be in a position of discovering my true self as 'Divine in Essence', with a separate identity from the physical body. When I identify myself with the soul which is immortal, the fear of death will automatically vanish. However, it is easier said than done and so I am still waiting for that moment to arrive.

The part the recollection of death plays in this respect is that it urges one to devote more and more time to meditation on God's Name with deep devotion and then to climb as many steps of the ladder of spiritual ascent as possible during this span of life. The main purpose of my life is finally to achieve union with God by working for it.

I do not look forward to death while waiting for it 'in the wings'. My attitude is summed up in what one great Sikh saint once told me: 'Never be afraid of death but never ask for it either.' Paradoxically, I have to be aware of it by remaining indifferent towards it.

Of course, I feel like talking about death with other people and sharing with them views, comments, apprehensions and fears. It will be all the more interesting to find out by which ways and means they try to conquer the fear of death. Being deeply imbued with my own Sikh tradition, I will naturally impress upon them the concept of immortality of soul and thus, that death is not to be seen as an end in itself. In this way they might see light and hope in life after death. Those who risk their life fighting for a righteous cause deserve our full sympathy and support in any way we may be able to offer them. I, for one, will hold sincere and heart-felt prayers for their success for the cause they hold so dear to themselves and for which they are prepared to risk their lives.

It is quite pertinent to mention here an episode from Guru Nanak's life story. Once, while approaching a town, he asked his all-time companion, Mardana, to go into the town and seek for an answer from the people to

103

the question: 'What is true and what is false?' He got all sorts of answers from different persons. One of the answers was 'To die is true and to live is false.' Guru was very much pleased with this answer, for it was correct. Whatever religion, race and colour we may belong to, we must recognise and accept the stark reality or truth in the above-mentioned answer, coming from a lay-person who was leading an unknown life.

A BUDDHIST PERSPECTIVE ON DEATH

Dr Peter Harvey, School of Humanities, Sunderland Polytechnic

Peter Harvey became a Buddhist whilst an undergraduate studying philosophy at Manchester University. He went on to Lancaster University to research into the Buddhist concept of 'person'. He now lectures on Eastern Religions at Sunderland Polytechnic and has recently published An Introduction to Buddhism *(Cambridge University Press, 1990). He is a Buddhist of the Theravada tradition and after several years of practising meditation now teaches Samantha meditation as part of the Samantha Trust, which has its national centre in Wales.*

Introduction

I write as a Western Buddhist, having come to Buddhism around nineteen years ago at the age of twenty, when I was at university. My reading on Buddhism introduced me to a system of thought which made much sense to me. The people who came to talk at a 'Buddhist Society' seemed to have qualities of calm and awareness that were admirable, and my introduction to the practice of meditation showed me a practical tool for developing such qualities. I am now a lecturer in Religious Studies and Philosophy, and also teach meditation. The tradition I follow is the Theravada school, and I base my practice

105

both on the early texts and a meditation tradition that comes from Thailand.

My perspective on death is informed by study of the Buddhist tradition, which makes more and more sense to me the further I explore it and reflect on the experience of living. Prior to moving into Buddhism, the Christian ideas which I had come across did not 'hang together' for me. In particular, the existence of suffering (including death) seemed (and still seems) incompatible with the idea that the world was created and is sustained by an all-loving, all-powerful being. Buddhism does not include such a view, but regards the world as a patterned process flowing on according to natural causes, with no discernible beginning in time. The present universe may have begun in a cosmic 'big bang', but what came 'before' that – a previous universe which shrank into itself? Whatever the proper scientific explanation may be, Buddhism focuses on understanding and dealing with the present flow of experience, with the aim of understanding, undermining and transcending the unsatisfactoriness (dukkha) which pervades life, doing this for oneself and helping others to do likewise. As such, life has no in-built purpose, it simply is as it is. But understanding the nature of life from a Buddhist perspective enables one to give one's life a purpose, rather than let it drift on from day to day, year to year, life to life.

The Buddha's Reflections on Death

In Buddhism, the inevitability of death is seen as a fruitful topic for reflection and meditation. Death was one of the 'four signs' that prompted Gotama (born c. 560BC and founder of the Buddhist religion) to leave his comfortable life as the son of a ruler to take up the life of a wandering ascetic in search of that which lay beyond all suffering. The later texts portray this renunciation of Gotama as arising from a sudden realisation rather than from a gradual reflection as it is represented in earlier texts. The Nidanakatha (a later sacred biography) relates that, on three consecutive days, Gotama visits one of his parks in his chariot. His father has the streets cleared of unpleasant sights, but the gods ensure that he sees a worn-out, grey-haired old man, a sick man and a corpse. As he is amazed at these new sights, his charioteer explains to him that ageing, sickness and death come to all people, thus putting him in a state of agitation at the nature of life. In this way, the texts portray an example of the human confrontation with frailty and mortality, for while these facts are theoretically 'known' to us all, a clear realisation and acceptance of them often does come as a novel and disturbing insight. On a fourth trip to his park, Gotama sees a saffron-robed religious mendicant with a shaved head and a calm demeanour, the sight of whom inspires him to adopt such a life-style for himself.

After a six-year quest, Gotama, at the age of thirty-five, attained a meditative breakthrough which meant that he was 'Enlightened' or 'Awakened': a Buddha. Key aspects of his Enlightenment experience are his memory of many of his previous rebirths, his observation of how beings are reborn according to the nature and quality of their karma (action), and a full realisation of Nirvana: that which is beyond suffering, change, conditionality, birth and death. Nirvana is a transforming, timeless experience, initially attained during life. At the passing away of an Enlightened person, there is then Nirvana beyond death.

Nirvana, whilst not seen as personal immortality, is seen as the 'Deathless': because it is also the 'Unborn'.

For whatever is subject to birth is also subject to death. Whatever arises – as a conditioned, limited, temporal phenomenon – also passes away, whether this be a passing feeling, the life of a living being, or a galaxy. To say that birth is a key cause of death may sound facile. But in a world-view which includes rebirth and the possibility of attaining the Deathless, it is a significant statement: if one can bring rebirth to an end, one will also transcend redeath, for repeated birth has brought, and will bring, repeated death in its train. Indeed, Buddhist teachers sometimes half seriously say that it is more 'sensible' to grieve at a birth and rejoice at a death than vice versa: the birth will lead to a future death, but the death is at least bringing one stretch of life and its sufferings to an end.

Death and Feelings of Solidarity With Others

Awareness of the inevitability of death can lead to a feeling of solidarity with other beings. Death 'levels' all: rich and poor, 'friend' and 'enemy', human and animal:

> As though huge mountains made of rock, so vast they reach up to the sky, were to advance from every side, grinding beneath them all that lives, so age and death roll over all. (Samyutta Nikăya:2)

All living beings, down to the insects that splat against my windscreen when I drive a car, desire to live, but sooner or later their life comes to an end. Reflections on the changes wrought by death and rebirth can also enhance respect for other beings. Thus, if some person or animal is presently annoying one, a way to undermine ill-will is to reflect that, in some past life, they must have been a close relative or friend, and have been very good to one (ibid. II.189–90). As Buddhism sees the chain of rebirth stretching back and back in time, with no discernible beginning, the law of averages means that we have crossed paths with all beings at some time. Similarly, any suffering that we now see others enduring will have been undergone by us in some previous life (ibid. II.186).

Rebirth and Karma

Death is not only seen as pertaining to humans and animals. It is endemic to all five kinds of rebirth realms: those of humans, animals, frustrated ghosts, hells and heavens. Whatever realm one is reborn in, death will come sooner or later. Even the gods die, to be reborn and die again.

Only the realisation of the Unborn, Nirvana, brings rebirth and redeath to an end. This realisation can be developed at the human level alone. The gods are generally too complacent and comfortable to be motivated to develop insight into such matters as impermanence; they also tend to think themselves immortal. In the realms of hell-beings, ghosts and animals, there is plenty of suffering of which to be aware, but beings must spend all their time dealing with it and have little freedom of action or thought. At the human level, there is enough suffering for it to be hard to ignore, but also sufficient freedom to develop insight into such matters and to grow spiritually.

As a broad generalisation, violence and hatred are seen as tending to a hellish rebirth; ignorance and delusion to rebirth as some kind of animal; strong attachment to rebirth as a ghost; generosity and virtue to rebirth as a human or lower god; and deep states of meditative calm to rebirth in the more refined heavens. None of this is seen as dependent on the will of a god; it is all regarded as working according to natural karmic laws. In this, actions (or rather the volitions underlying them) are like seeds, which will naturally develop into a certain kind of fruit.

Understandably, the question arises: should modern Buddhists take talk of 'rebirth' literally? Did early Buddhism simply take the idea of reincarnation/rebirth for granted, absorbing it from Indian culture? Should it be interpreted metaphorically? I would answer 'no' to these questions. At the time of the Buddha, rebirth and karma were relatively new ideas but the early Buddhist texts portray the Buddha as having taught karma and rebirth because he felt that he had good evidence for them – based on extensive meditative experience – and not just because it was a common idea. In response to the sceptics and materialists, he taught that it is possible to know from experience that karma and rebirth are realities (Majjhima Nikāya: 402).

On the matter of seeing rebirth as metaphorical, one influential Thai monk, Buddhadasa, emphasises the idea that rebirth is to be observed within life: as the birth and death, arising and passing away of sensations, moods and ego feelings. As regards rebirth as pertaining to what happens at the end of a life, he seems to be agnostic. Such a view is also found among some Western Buddhists. It should be said, though, that it is a somewhat imbalanced view. Traditional teaching already included the idea that 'rebirth' pertains both to the start of a new life and the start of a new moment of existence within a life. Thus to see a 'this life', 'non-literal' interpretation as in competition with a more 'traditional' one is inappropriate. The doctrine is about both moment-to-moment and life-to-life change.

For most Buddhists, 'rebirth' will only function as a belief, a belief that makes much sense of life, but a belief none the less. The Buddha taught that people should not be attached to beliefs and views, even those advocated by himself. Getting hot under the collar about 'my beliefs' is a form of attachment which leads to suffering and to quarrels. The aim is, ultimately, to know for oneself what is true, by direct (meditative) experience. Most people have not yet developed this ability, however, and so must work with the idea of rebirth as an eminently sensible hypothesis which provides a framework that helps orientate them in life. They may also cite, in support of this hypothesis, the accurate descriptions that some young children can give of the lives of deceased people they claim to have been.

Death, Rebirth and Motivation

One importance of working with a rebirth perspective is that it provides part of the basis for long-term motivation for moral and spiritual practice. While death means that one loses all physical possessions, and is parted from one's loved ones and one's life's 'attainments', the purification of character that is developed by ethical and meditative practice is seen as something that death does not destroy. It becomes part of one's mental continuum that will 'spill over' into another life. In that life, the spiritual development of this life may be neglected or further built on; but, at the very least, it can act as a positive residue of this life to be used as a foundation for further development. In the Tibetan tradition there is, indeed, a series of reflections to help motivate spiritual practice. The first concerns the rarity of human life. Given the other forms of rebirth, and that there are many more animals (including birds, fishes, insects, etc.) than humans, being born as a human is a rare precious opportunity for spiritual improvement.

Therefore, one should apply oneself to spiritual practice now, for the benefit that this will bring both to oneself and others. Verses from the Dhammapada which also encourage this attitude are as follows:

> The man of little (spiritual) learning grows old like a bull: his muscles grow, his wisdom grows not. (Dhammapada: 152)

> They who have not led the Holy Life, who in youth have not acquired wealth, pine away like herons on a pond without fish. (ibid. 155)

> As from a heap of flowers many a garland is made, even so many good deeds should be done by one born mortal. (ibid. 53)

> His good deeds will receive the doer who has gone from this world to the next, as kinsmen will receive a dear one on his return. (ibid. 220)

Meditation on Death

In beginning this meditation, it is seen as inappropriate to dwell on the death of a friend, an enemy, a neutral person or oneself, as this might lead, respectively, to sorrow, gladness, indifference, and anxiety, not to a calm heart which will result in the practice of good works. Thus the meditator should commence by dwelling on past deaths of people who had enjoyed a pleasant life. Then the mind of the meditator can be turned to the inevitability of his or her own death, so as to develop one-pointed concentration on this. To aid this are various reflections, such as:

The nights and days go slipping by,
As life keeps dwindling steadily
Till mortals' span, like water pools
In failing rills, is all used up.
(Samyutta Nikăya: I.: 109)

Death comes to oneself just as it comes to those of great fame, strength and understanding. Many are the possible causes of death, be they external causes or the small organisms with which one shares one's body. Life is frail; it will end if one lacks air to breathe or food to eat, or if the body is either too hot or too cold. Death is unpredictable as to the age at which one may die, at what time of day, of what, and where. One may live only another day . . . or for the time it takes to eat a meal . . . or chew the next mouthful . . . or take the next breath – but one should use whatever time one has to rouse energy and mindfulness for spiritual practice. Insight into impermanence and non-attachment to life will then develop, and a person will die without fear.

As regards myself, I realise that it is likely that I will one day die of a heart attack, as heart disease runs in my family. A couple of years ago, I bought a digital watch, which had programmed into it the day of the week for any date over the next hundred years. It struck me that it therefore had in it the day and date of my death. (Watches 'die' too, though, and this one 'died' before I did!) My meditation practice includes calming concentration on the breath, loving-kindness meditation, and reflection on impermanence, suffering and not-self (that no substantial, permanent self can be found in the flow of conditioned mental and physical states that 'I' am). In the latter 'insight' practice, reflection on death can be part of contemplation of suffering. I therefore try calmly to contemplate my own ageing and death and any feelings

113

that are generated, along with the deaths of loved ones who are presently alive. This, too, can generate considerable feeling, but the aim is calmly to contemplate such feeling, as a way of coming to terms with the realities of life, and learning from them. This also means that dealing with the death of a loved one can begin before it happens; it is a kind of prophylaxis, a way of preparing your system. As regards contemplating my own death, this is a very good way of generating vigour, so as not to waste my life but to take the opportunity that a human life gives for spiritual development.

Contemplation of death is not morbid if it is done from the right perspective. Thoughts of death are only morbid if one generally tries to avoid them, and feels heavy and low when one's ignorance of death cannot be sustained in a certain situation. Living with an awareness of one's death helps one to live life better, and also prepares one for dying well. I do not myself find death a difficult thing to talk about. In our family, talk may concern death, rebirth and karma as much as many other things. Neither my wife nor my daughter see it as an unpleasant or embarrassing subject. However, I have never had an opportunity to talk of death with someone who is terminally ill, or in a dangerous profession. Nor have I had an opening to talk of death with one who is particularly afraid of it.

Dying and the Time Before Rebirth

Within limits set by a person's karma the state of mind in which he or she dies is a key determinant of what kind of rebirth follows. Relatives of the dying thus seek to facilitate a 'good death'. The dying person will be reminded of his past good deeds, so as to rejoice at these; he will also be invited to participate mentally in the good deed of feeding monks. A calm and uplifted state will be encouraged by the monks' chanting.

In Tibetan tradition, someone may read the Tibetan Book of the Dead (Bardo Thotrol) to a dying person to prepare him or her for the experiences that follow death. This reading continues after the death of the body, as it is envisaged that the dead person's consciousness is still able to benefit from the reading. The contents of the Tibetan Book of the Dead recount that a person will encounter a brilliant light at death (compare contemporary literature on near-death experiences), which is seen as the 'clear light of the void', a direct vision of ultimate reality. Most people are seen as flinching away from this, being unable fully to 'take' it. They are thus then subject to a variety of visionary experiences in the 'intermediary existence' between rebirths. Depending on their level of understanding, they may actually be able to attain Enlightenment in this period, or at least influence the level of their rebirth.

As regards the question of whether an 'intermediary existence' does intervene between rebirths, the traditions of Buddhism differ. The Theravada school, which is the dominant one in Sri Lanka and South-East Asia, holds that rebirth is instantaneous: the moment of death is immediately followed by the moment of conception in the next life. The Mahayana tradition, found in Tibetan cultural areas, and in East Asia, accepts an 'intermediary existence'. However, my reading of the Theravada collection of early texts is such that I detect an acceptance in them of an 'intermediary existence'. I envisage such a time as a period of searching for a new existence, driven by the continued grasping at life, and as a period of readjustment. The Mahayana tradition envisages it as lasting from seven to forty-nine days.

As regards the reference to a bright light being experienced after death, I can relate this to Theravadin ideas on the nature of the dying consciousness, which is seen as a form of bhavanga, the resting state of consciousness, which flows uninterruptedly in dreamless sleep. This in turn is equated with the 'brightly shining mind' (Aṅguttara Nikaya:I:10), the depth aspect of the mind which is endowed with loving-kindness.

Funerals and Memorials

My own first real experience was when my father died of a heart attack one morning. I remember pleading with him, by then unconscious, not to die. He was fifty and I was seventeen and not yet a Buddhist. Immediately after he had died, I found I could not cry, not being an emotional person, but I guess that I've let emotion out since.

Other deaths that I have experienced have been those of my aunt, and my wife's nephew who died in 1987 from an accident in which he was crushed by a road-roller while working on a road. His was the first burial that I had been to. Buddhists generally choose cremation, as a way of clearly acknowledging the finality of death. However, I found that the way that cremations are done in our culture, burials are in fact much more 'real'. In crematoriums, the coffin sinks down or slides behind some curtains and that is the last one sees of it. In watching a coffin being lowered into a grave, there appears to be a much clearer 'transition' signalling the end of life, though of course for the mourners the experience can be more painful. However, relatives may sometimes then become attached to the grave and act as if the person is still alive there.

At Buddhist funerals in Sri Lanka, the following verse is printed on sheets of paper and posted all over a village:

> *All conditioned things are impermanent;*
> *Their nature is to arise and pass away.*
> *They come into being only to be destroyed;*
> *Their cessation is bliss.*

These are words said to have been uttered by a god at the death of the Buddha. The 'bliss' is not death as such, but the attainment of Nirvana. The deceased person's name is also printed on the sheets, along with an aspiration such as 'May he find the blissful peace of Nirvana'. That is, may he in some future life attain that which transcends birth and death. At the funeral, monks often give a sermon dwelling on impermanence and the inevitability of death. The Salla Sutta (Sutta-nipara: 574–93) is often a theme. This includes the verses:

So death and ageing are endemic to the world.
Therefore the wise do not grieve,
Seeing the nature of the world (ibid. 581)

So we can listen and learn from the noble man as he gives up his grief.
When he sees that someone has passed away and lived out their life,
He says 'he will not be seen by me again.' (ibid. 590)

Grief is seen as a perfectly natural human feeling, and should not be repressed; but nor should it be especially dwelt on or stimulated. At the death of the

117

Buddha, the unenlightened grieved but the Enlightened acknowledged that all conditioned phenomena must come to an end.

I have never been to a Buddhist funeral, but someone I know who went to the funeral of his meditation teacher's wife said that his teacher urged those at the funeral not to be so miserable – that his wife had lived a good life, and that there was nothing to feel heavy about. At Christian funeral ceremonies, I just sing along with whatever words of the hymns hold any meaning for me.

As regards mourning, perhaps the most relevant thing is the idea of doing good deeds on behalf of the dead person, soon after their death, to boost their stock of 'merit', or good karma. Chanting by monks at the funeral may also have a calming effect on the consciousness of the dead person, and help them in their quest for their next life.

All Buddhist traditions envisage that 'transference of merit' is a way of actually benefiting the dead. For it to work, the dead person must mentally participate in and rejoice at a good deed that one does on their behalf. Strictly speaking, the dead can only benefit from such 'transference' or 'sharing' if they are reborn as ghosts. It may be that a particular relative is reborn in some other realm, but there will always be some ancestors in the ghost realm, who can benefit from 'merit' transfer.

Some years after my father's death, I conducted a small memorial service, asking a monk I knew for a meal and dedicating the 'merit' to my father. The monk asked me to show him a photo of my father, and after the 'dana' (giving), he did some chanting, while pouring water in a vessel till it overflowed, symbolising the sharing of 'merit'. In this small way, I felt that I might be doing something to help my father.

Thoughts on My Own Death

My thoughts and attitudes to my own death (can death be 'mine', be owned?) are as follows.

If I do not die without warning, I envisage that the prospect of death, and associated pain, will stimulate deep-rooted attachments and fears. Certainly I do not 'look forward' to death, nor am I indifferent to it. It will end a human existence, with all its opportunities for spiritual development, and also many ordinary pleasures, to which I am attached in varying degrees! To the extent that I have 'got myself together' by previous meditative practice, I would hope that I could master these feelings to some extent, in the sense of letting them arise and pass away without repressing them or being perturbed by them. Clearly, it would be good to be able to talk to my family about my death, for mutual comfort and to be able to leave things for them as well as I could. I would hope to be able to use the dying process as a time for deepening spiritual practice and learning. I guess that the moment of actual death would be facilitated by a letting go of life and concerns for what was going on around one. Literature on the near-death experience (NDE) suggests that, close to death, there would be an out-of-the-body experience, entailing looking down at 'my' dying or dead body. Then might come an experience of going down a tunnel towards a benevolent light, which I would see as an experience of the benevolent depth-aspect of the mind.

A rapid review of life's experience and deeds might then be expected, as recorded in the NDE literature. I can relate this to the Buddhist idea that images linked to one's actions (karmas) in life flash before one at death. Prior to moving on to the next rebirth (assuming I don't manage to attain Nirvana in the present life!), I envisage a period of wandering in search of a suitable environment for birth. As to how I would be reborn, well, that depends on my back-log karma, both from this present life and previous ones.

Regarding whether 'I' will continue after death, I go along with the Buddhist perspective concerning all phenomena as being devoid of a permanent substantial self. What 'I' (this conditioned stream of mental and physical processes) will become will be a development from and beyond what 'I' am now. From life to life, a being is neither identically the same nor entirely different (Milandpañha: 40). Character patterns may persist, but these will gradually change. As it is, one is constantly changing within one life, so death will just be a more marked change in the continuity of mental and physical states that a 'being' is. Therefore 'my' death cannot be seen as important in the wider perspective. As such, death is an event shared in only by the dying person, their friends and relatives, and those who have some connection with them. It entails a final parting (though one may cross paths again in the future), in which the dying person must leave the world alone, and leave the gap which he or she has left to close up. Those who are left must wish the 'journeyer' well and say goodbye.

For me, death acts as a reminder to use the spiritual opportunities of human life wisely, while one is still able to; it reminds one of karma, and to avoid evil and do good; it produces compassion for others and feelings of solidarity for other living/dying beings; it reminds one that death is dependent on birth, and that only the Unborn is Deathless. It also reminds one of impermanence in general, and that we are 'born' and 'die' each moment.

DEATH

Professor Sir Hermann Bondi, Master of Churchill College, Cambridge

Hermann Bondi was born in Vienna and educated there and at Trinity College, Cambridge. After a distinguished career as a mathematician and astrophysicist (he had previously held the chair of Mathematics at King's College, London) Hermann Bondi returned to Cambridge to become the Master of Churchill College, an appointment he held until 1990. Since the early 1950s he has been involved in the Humanist movement and is the President of the British Humanist Association and of the Rationalist Press Association. He is married and has five children and four grandchildren.

I find it difficult to get excited about the alleged philosophical problems of death, for death, as the ending of life, is to me an utterly natural phenomenon. I cannot see any way of detaching mental processes from the physical ones of the body. My most abstract mathematical thoughts seem to me in no way different in kind from those relating to hunger or to sexual desire. Equally, my most ethereal pleasures, of music or mountain views, are so totally linked to physical processes of hearing and seeing that I cannot conceive of their having any independent significance. Thus any idea of life after death seems to me to be meaningless.

One of the greatest features of nature's life processes is the arising of new life. This is certainly a most joyful event for us followed by the intriguing development of growing up amongst humans, and something that touches a deep chord in us also when we observe it in other animals. It seems to me absurd to conceive of a situation in which wholly novel individuals arrive through birth, while the old are not equally totally removed through death. Thus birth and death seem to me two sides of the same coin.

To regard death as natural in no way implies that it is pleasant. After all, to be thirsty when it is hot is wholly natural yet distinctly unpleasant.

That my own life will come to an end is something with which I have no quarrel. To think of my death in the distant future evokes no particular feelings in me; to think of it in the relatively near future produces considerable feelings of serious irritation at all the jobs left unfinished, at all the experience I have gathered that will now be useless, at letting down all those to whom I am tied by love and friendship, and all who rely on me for help and advice. Of course, this attitude has changed in character over the years. As a very young man I was most bothered about my friends and about the contributions to my academic subject that would not be made if I died too soon. A little later I was horrified at the thought of leaving my wife and children without husband and father, while in the next stage, with major managerial responsibilities, I was very conscious that my death would make many people, rightly, feel anxious and let down. Now that I am yet older, my feelings in contemplating death are less those arising from responsibilities and more of regret at not seeing my children's lives develop and those of my grandchildren unfolding, followed by irritation at not being able to do more travelling, walking, and above all seeing things coming next.

Yet all these cool calculations are not much in my mind when danger suddenly appears and I am simply terrified! The strength of this animal emotion of deep fear can be quite surprising.

As for the manner of my death, my reactions are those of one who, along with his close family, has been fortunate to enjoy excellent health. To have to be in hospital horrifies me; to die in the heavy atmosphere of a sick room I find too repulsive to contemplate. Thus I very much hope for a sudden death, while I still enjoy good health. An accident or a sudden failure of circulation would be most acceptable. I have built so much of my personal life and of my career on being fit and untiring that the idea of being helpless and weak is most disagreeable to me.

Naturally I recognise that we are not all the same. Nothing is to me more admirable than a person who overcomes a physical handicap to lead a truly full life, interacting forcefully and well with other people. This is making a great contribution to all of us, especially so by setting such a wonderful example for others, whether fit or handicapped.

What is at the other end of the scale is a decline of mental powers that can reduce a person's interaction with others to very low levels, indeed effectively to zero in the dreaded 'vegetable' condition in which modern medicine can keep one formally alive. I doubt, though, whether such an existence can honestly be termed living, for to me life must involve strong human linkages. This unhappily not uncommon decline is a spectre that hangs over all of us, and I for one would very much like to avoid it.

Choosing one's moment for going is no doubt very difficult, but I would be prepared to pay a high price to avoid a long period of physical and especially mental incapacity. It might be worth saying that while these last thoughts have naturally come more towards the centre of my thinking as I have grown older, my attitude in general has not changed for as long as I can remember.

As a Humanist I believe in the importance of human linkages, of human interactions, of our lives getting their meaning from our connections with each other. Thus I agree with Donne ('Meditation XVII') that anybody's death diminishes us all. Yet our loss, our grief, our sorrow at matters that have been left unsaid for too long, services that we regret not having performed in time, and the sheer feeling of void must all be seen in proportion, difficult as this may be. If a person dies in ripe old age, after a life that has had more ups than downs, a life that was at least in some sense fulfilling, then one's grief should surely be limited in duration, if not in depth. The very naturalness of death, the fact that it is unavoidable, should reconcile one gradually to what has happened in such cases. But if a young, fit person dies, then the grief, the horror, yes, the anger at the event cannot easily be bounded. To have to remain for ever ignorant of how the one who died would have lived, to realise that we must all manage without the unique contribution that person could have made to society, all this may border on the unbearable. One cannot compare the limitless grief over a life that has not yet unfolded to the feeling of loss over one that has gone in the fullness of time.

Yet with all my horror of young people dying I would not wish, even if I could, to wrap them in cotton wool. The young (and not only the young) are rightly adventurous, rightly willing to take risks, and I would not wish it otherwise. Such risks, undergone in the necessary and desirable enterprise of gaining experience, say, in climbing mountains, are bound occasionally to lead to a death. One's sense of loss will be just as great, yet such a tragedy, arising out of a willingly and purposefully faced danger, is not as hard to bear as death due to a senseless motor accident or randomly striking disease.

The extreme case of risk faced for a purpose is war. In my own lifetime the Second World War took place. There was never a doubt in my mind that it was necessary, and this made the loss of friends and colleagues no less grievous, but not quite so hard to bear.

This leads me to a comment addressed to those who are unenthusiastic about the high standard of living now attained throughout the industrialised world and gradually approached by the populations of some, at least, of the developing countries. These people claim that our advances are only relative, that one could have been just as happy in an earlier poorer age. I profoundly disagree. It is said that 150 years ago it was common in an artisan's household to have a child's coffin under the kitchen table, for one or more of the children were bound to die young, and it was financially sound to make provision for this in good time. Thanks to our standard of living, to good housing, to plenty of hot water, to clean water, to hygienically prepared food, to inoculations, to less-polluted air, almost all children survive now. Many matters indeed are relative, and 'absolute' is a difficult term but to me the great reduction in the numbers of parents who have to grieve for a child is as absolute a good as comes into my vocabulary.

To aim to avoid death altogether is silly, to work to banish premature death is a noble aim.

DEATH

The Revd Professor Frances M. Young,
Cadbury Professor of Theology,
University of Birmingham

*Frances Young has taught theology at Birmingham
University since the 1970s and in 1977 contributed
to the volume of essays* The Myth of God Incarnate
(SCM Press), *edited by the then Wood Professor of
Theology, John Hick. In 1986 she was appointed to the
Edward Cadbury Chair of Theology and became head
of the School of Philosophy and Theology in 1989. She
was ordained into the Methodist Ministry in 1984. Her
publications include studies in the Christian Doctrine
of the Atonement and work on the Early Fathers. She
is married and has three sons, the eldest of whom is
severely handicapped.*

The question of death and what it means cannot be
considered in isolation. My attitude to death relates to
my sense of what 'I' am, and also to my response to what
other people are and the effect on me of their death, or
potential death. Nor can I address the question as if I
had reached a conclusion which will remain permanent.
To explain my present views means telling the story of
how I got them, and if my account gets fixed and then
stops, there is something wrong with me. To live to the
full means being open to change and to think I'd got it
all taped would be a kind of death.

As a youngster growing up in the Methodist Church, I assimilated the popular Christian picture of the soul going to heaven when you die, where you'll be with Jesus, and the body decaying in the tomb (or burning in the crematorium). In a sense the soul was the 'real me' and the body and its disposal was relatively irrelevant. This outlook was confirmed by an early experience of bereavement. My brother died at the age of sixteen, just before I left home for university. It was both a dreadful experience of loss, and an experience of assurance that God was real and that death could not be the end, both joy and sorrow at a peculiarly intense level. It also initiated a process of profound questioning about life and its purpose: my brother had felt called to the ministry, but God had not let him live – why? I still have no answer, but find it puzzling and intriguing that my own life has led me first into theology and then into ordination as a Methodist Minister; only afterwards and by hindsight did I realise I had somehow fulfilled his destiny.

Chronologically, the next step in my thinking about death was an academic discovery, but it was one that rang increasingly true as life's experiences proceeded. As a student of theology, I discovered that the idea of the soul's immortality derived from Plato and the traditions of Greek philosophy, and it simply is not in the Bible. The Judaeo-Christian tradition at the biblical stage developed a very different notion, the resurrection of the body, and in the early centuries of Christianity this idea was opposed to the pagan doctrine of the soul's immortality by Christian apologists. Only later was the Greek philosophical idea integrated into popular as well as more sophisticated Christian schemes of belief. The significance of this probably needs a little more exploration.

If you examine the Hebrew Bible, you will discover

that the idea of death expressed there is a purely naturalistic one. The creation of a human being according to
Genesis 2 meant the creature being formed of clay, the
dust of the earth, and coming alive by God's Spirit being
breathed into it. A similar picture is implied by Ezekiel's
famous vision of the dry bones (37:1–14): the prophet is
asked, 'Can these dry bones live?' then told to prophesy
to the bones: first the bones come rattling together into
skeletons, then sinews, flesh and skin cover them, and
life comes when God's breath or Spirit is breathed into
them. God is the source of all life, which is sheer gift.
Death means the end, the dissolution of the creature,
the return to dust. This view is found all over the
Hebrew Bible, in the Psalms, in what we call the
'Wisdom Literature' (Job, Proverbs, Ecclesiastes), as well
as being assumed in the historical narratives. Here are
some examples:

> Lord, let me know my end
> and what is the measure of my days . . .
> Surely every man stands as a mere breath
> Surely man goes about as a shadow . . .
> Look away from me, that I may know gladness,
> before I depart and *be no more*.
>> (Ps. 39:4–5 and 13)

> As for man, his days are like grass;
> he flourishes like a flower of the field;
> for the wind passes over it and it is gone,
> and its place knows it no more.
>> (Ps. 103:15–16)

> For now I shall lie in the earth;
> thou will seek me, but *I shall not be*.
>> (Job 7:21)

> Though his height mount up to the heavens . . .
> he will perish for ever like his own dung;
> His bones are full of youthful vigour,
> but it will lie down and him in the dust.
>
> (Job 20:6–7 and 11)

> For the fate of the sons of men and the fate of
> beasts is the same; as one dies, so dies the
> other. They all have the same breath, and man
> has no advantage over the beasts . . . All go to
> one place; all are from the dust, and all turn
> to dust again.
>
> (Eccles. 3:19–20)

Alongside this naturalistic view, however, we find references to Sheol as the place of the dead. Sometimes the name simply refers to the grave, thus confirming the naturalistic view; but more often it refers to an underworld not unlike Hades in Greek mythology. To Sheol a 'shade' or ghost of the former person would descend at death. Sheol is a land of darkness (Job 10:21), a land of rest, sleep and forgetfulness – the dead know nothing (Eccles. 9:5); some texts suggest that the dead continue the functions they performed in life, but they have no real life – a shadowy existence like a dream. Sheol is the land of silence (Ps. 94:17); in Sheol there is no praising of God, and God remembers the dead no more (Ps. 88). Saul is described as calling up the ghost of Samuel from Sheol (1 Sam. 28) but necromancy was forbidden by the Law (Deut. 18:11): such details confirm the general picture. Sheol and death induced feelings of utter hopelessness and were associated with the *absence* of God who was the source of real full-blooded life. Psalm 139:8, 'If I make my bed in Sheol, thou art there!' is quite exceptional: generally God's power was not thought to reach to the underworld, though he could prevent you getting there. If you look closely, you will observe that many Psalms pray for escape from death, by healing from sickness or rescue from enemies. There is no hint, however, of the possibility of survival *after* death, or of death's reversal.

Nevertheless, revival from death became a powerful image of Israel's national restoration after the exile in Ezekiel's famous vision of the dry bones, and this no doubt helped to stimulate the view that God's power could extend to the realm of the dead, and he might restore the dead to life. Prior to New Testament times, some Jewish groups (certainly the Pharisees but not the Sadducees) had come to believe that the wrongs and injustices of this world would be put right in a new creation to which the dead would be *raised*; God would give them back their life at the End of the World. Often coupled with this was the notion of a final judgement, so both just and wicked would be raised from the dead to get their deserts. A few passages, in what Christians call the Old Testament, which are of late date, reflect this view. 'Resurrection of the body' meant God's creative power to bring the dead back to life, and implied a very different outlook from 'immortality of the soul'.

There's no need to go further into Ancient Near Eastern mythology. The point is that when I was a student, the biblical idea of human nature was opposed to the Platonic idea, with the implication that Christianity should reclaim its biblical theology, Hellenic ideas being foreign imports. This meant, firstly, regarding a human being as a psychosomatic unity, a single being not a being made up of two components, soul and body; and secondly, treating death as a natural end of life, but not necessarily one's personal end, since God could restore one to life, and if one was 'in Christ', would do so. The important thing was that there was no 'soul' with an inbuilt 'immortality':

131

life was God's gift and depended wholly upon him. This view was regarded as significant since it cohered with 'modern' views of human nature. Philosophy, psychology, the biological sciences, etc., had rejected the soul-body understanding, and the naturalistic view of the Bible was therefore more coherent as a belief system in the modern context. It also put the stress on God's will and purpose to create and give life, and was therefore more theologically powerful. For me it was confirmed by life.

The 'ghost in the machine' view of myself ceased to be attractive or convincing. There is a real sense in which 'I am my body'. The most dramatic demonstration of this was the experience of giving birth to a baby; my physical being and me simply could not be separated. Years later I attempted to express this in a poem:

Body Awareness

Physical I was made
Physical I am
I feel I am
Physical.
I glory in being

Lying in a bath
Soaking up the warmth
Strained body relaxed
Soothed, caressed and nursed
Blood tingling in every vein
Joy tingling in every nerve
Thanks mingling with every thought.

Lying in a bath
Breathing in hot steam

Weary muscles relieved
Torn flesh cleansed and healed
Milk tingling in swollen breasts
Joy tingling in every nerve
Thanks mingling with every thought.

Lying in a bath
Revelling in new birth
Purged of pain's assault
Re-integrated self
Love tingling in every pore
Joy tingling in every nerve
Thanks mingling with every thought.

Physical I was made.
Physical I am.
I feel I am
Physical.
I glory in being
Physical.
I taste the spiritual
Within the physical.

(First published in *Foundation*, Autumn 1984 – the magazine of the Westminster Pastoral Foundation.)

The poem actually came to me years later, as I've indicated, when soaking in a bath after a five-mile run. For here, too, I discovered how spiritual exaltation accompanies physical exhilaration. And there is the opposite effect; depression and loss of morale sap physical energy. In a very real sense, I am my body – as a matter of experience, and not just because modern biological science or psychology tells me so.

The second thing that happened to confirm the psychosomatic unity of a human being was having to live with and grow with the reality of a severely handicapped son. His brain never developed properly because of deprivation of oxygen in the womb. It is clear that his entire personality is bound by the limitations of that one central physical organ. I cannot gaze into his eyes and imagine the 'real Arthur' inside the physical shell – for years we didn't even have much eye contact. He is what he is, and what he is is a physical being, with a genetic inheritance, an environment of influences, and the devastating limitations of a damaged brain which could not respond to either his genetic inheritance or those external influences in the normal way. So his personality has not developed normally; what person there is is incapable of speech, and it is hard to imagine what his thought-processes are like since he lacks language. I can't envisage what his 'soul' might be. Yet he is human, and he responds not just to physical needs, but to human fellowship with smiles, laughter, tears and screams. He is as he is, and his real self is a physical matter.

The third thing that undermined the soul-body dualism was the experience of living with my father-in-law for the last five years of his life, and watching a person become a non-person as he succumbed to Parkinson's disease. That may seem to express it rather harshly, and certainly it is to put it in an extreme way – but the physical deterioration of part of his brain gradually brought about not only a physical deterioration in his bodily functions, but also in his personality. Just as I am my body, and my son is his body, so my father-in-law was his body. I began to hope I'd pop off at sixty rather than live on to deteriorate and cease to be myself.

So for me, death became a natural part of life, if a somewhat distressing one. Just like the leaves in the autumn, so also animals, including human mammals, have their natural term, their natural end. This being so, I find the taboo about the death in modern society unnatural and unhealthy. I have no problems about discussing it openly and expressing views which others find controversial where it is appropriate. Although for several years, especially under the impact of the questions raised by my son's condition, my hold on faith was a bit tenuous, this view of death did not in fact appear incompatible with Christianity. It was, as I've explained, entirely biblical; and at my grandmother's death, despite tragic years of increasing senility whose poignancy made me weep with despair at this mortal life, I experienced a similar assurance in bereavement as I had when my brother died, joy as well as sorrow, since God seemed very real, and I knew she was safe in the everlasting arms. That was enough; it didn't matter that I found myself entirely agnostic about how that might be. What had happened was a fundamental shift of emphasis away from some idea of automatic survival (the immortality of the soul) to absolute, if somewhat agnostic, trust in God.

Over the years, these two convictions have become the pedal notes on which variations are played: death is the natural end and God is love. There was a long black period in which my handicapped son was rarely happy, and often cried for hour after hour, refusing to be comforted. If you put an animal out of its misery through sheer compassion, why couldn't we relieve him in the same way? Death is part of natural life. Why the taboo? Why does society and medical success *prevent* him dying?

In an earlier period of history, he would probably never have survived into adulthood. Nature and its Creator are more compassionate than humanity, I felt.

The rigid principle 'Life is sacred' is a humanistic view, not a specifically Christian one. I became bitterly angry with the *Life* organisation, and rejoiced to read that their victim, Dr Arthur, was reading the Bible in the dock. (He was brought to trial for 'assisting' the death of a baby with Down's syndrome and other handicaps.) After a number of easier years in which I've been able to give thanks for my son, years when my anguish seemed resolved, I now find myself more and more frequently praying again that he will not live much longer. I should mourn, grieve, miss him more than I can say. But I dread what the future holds for him, and long for a compassionate end. Increasingly, I am confident that 'all will be well, all manner of things will be well' (*Revelations of Divine Love*, Lady Julian of Norwich), because I somehow trust the love of God more and more deeply. But I don't really know how things will be well, and I certainly don't believe that some ideal unhandicapped Arthur will persist and everything will be put right in the next life. The pedal notes remain; death is the natural end, and God is love.

Over that ground, certain tunes persistently play. One is the importance of our selves as members of a community. If the love of God is fundamental, then our love for one another is the overspill of an infinite ocean of love, and it is an important pointer to a kind of transcendence. So my belonging to Christ involves the inarticulate belonging of my son, and of others who belong to me but may not share my faith. I can't believe that the fullness of life and love we share is to be annihilated. It seems an anticipation of an even fuller life and love which will be God's gift to us if we are attuned to receive it. How that will be we can only imagine in symbols and images – the favourite picture of God's Kingdom in the Bible being a wedding-feast or a party:

A party invitation! the heavenly feast!
Who'll be there?
Everyone's invited, even the least.
I've nothing to wear . . .
A special robe is provided, designed for you.
Look at my hair!
Don't worry – they'll give you a bath and a
*   fine hair-do.*
No gift to bear . . .
Just bring your musical instrument to play.
Arthur can't share.
Everyone will participate in some way.
Stuck in his chair?
Somehow he'll be fitted to play his role.
Will people stare?
No, no. He'll take his part in the joyful whole.
He'll be aware?
Everyone will respond and give of their best.
*   Each has some flair.*
*   The conductor, you see, will be a special guest.*
*   Under his care*
*   The entire ensemble will play together as one.*
That'll be rare.
That is how Christ will complete the work begun
*   Suffering in prayer.*
*   There'll be music beyond any music heard on*
*   earth*
*   Throbbing the air.*
*   There'll be bread and wine. New life will be*
*   brought to birth.*
*   God will be there.*
You'll finally understand his infinite grace.
*   There's plenty to spare.*
Will we be able to see him face to face?
Look – if you dare!

(First published in *Face to Face*, 1985.)

Another theme is the sense that intimations of God in this life, and the painful experiences of 'judgement' when we see ourselves as we really are, are anticipations of a deeper awareness, part of a process of preparation for a reality which we can barely imagine. Heaven and hell are images for the beauty and awe-fulness of finding ourselves in God's presence, something expressed most powerfully for me in Elgar's setting of the *Dream of Gerontius*. But I cannot believe in hell as eternal punishment for the wicked – God cannot be that sadistic. If death is part of the natural processes of the Creation, then I guess that those not attuned in any way to receive God's transcendent life will simply die – fade out and disintegrate, like the flower of the field: dust to dust, ashes to ashes. In that sense, the wages of sin is death. Nor can I believe that our responsiveness is measured in terms of doctrinal orthodoxy. The sayings of Jesus suggest that response to God and to the beauty and goodness of the life he has created is a much more paradoxical matter than our single human categorisations of good and evil, truth and falsehood. People who are deeply true to themselves, responsive to the mystery of life, to the natural world and other people, appreciative and generous, who are unconscious and even agnostic saints, are nearer to God than the avowedly religious of any faith, including Christians, who often bear the characteristics of the Pharisees Jesus criticised. The deepest sin is that distorted vision which calls evil good and good evil, and acts accordingly. To such sin in ourselves we are usually blind. That is the sin against the Holy Spirit which is unforgivable, quite simply because we cannot repent of it as long as our blindness persists.

I am deeply attracted to 'universalism', the view that in the end God will save everyone, but this has the same problems as belief in the immortality of the soul: it seems too automatic. I am more and more convinced that God's grace and love are fundamental, but that such grace and love allow others to be what they choose to be, and like a loving parent, God has to 'let go' or his love becomes coercion. This is part of the pain of loving, and God's pain is demonstrated for me in the suffering of Christ on the Cross. His power is a kind of weakness, his acceptance that his love may be flouted. He pays the penalty for risking a creation of free beings rather than automata, taking the responsibility for it upon himself and sharing in the pain of it. We cannot therefore guarantee that all will be saved, for some may never respond. For some, death really is the end.

No – that way of putting it reduces the significance of death. For all, death really is the end. Religious belief has tended to reduce its significance by treating it as though it were only a kind of sleep from which we shall assuredly waken. Rejection of the idea of the automatic immortality of the soul means rejecting the idea that this life is *merely* preparation. This life is to be affirmed and lived to the full, and this world is to be acclaimed as God's great Creation. To establish this, the Church fought its first battle against heresy. Christianity is *not* fundamentally an 'other-worldly' religion. But if this life is primary, we cannot avoid the conclusion that death is the end, and the mysterious cycle of nature whereby new life grows on the dead matter of past existences can only be treated as a parable. Yet it *is* a parable of death and resurrection, and even if death is the end for me as an individual, God's creative purposes do not end. Ultimately, his purpose and love alone are the basis of trust and hope. He will grant new life. But what form that new life will take, and exactly how 'I' and those I love will participate in it, can only be a mystery.

But my pilgrimage goes on, as I said at the beginning.

As I grow older, I begin to be aware of death beginning in life. Bits of my body are removed by dentist or surgeon, and yet 'I' am not violated. The role of the physical in my relationship with my husband changes, and I know there is much more than that in our love. I seem not wholly identified with my body after all. Yet my body still affects me profoundly; it is sometimes a drag, and physical exhilaration from exercise is unlikely to go on facilitating mental and spiritual exaltation. I dread the loss of mental powers which so often accompanies physical decay; I'm not afraid of death, but I am desperately afraid of the process of dying. Consciousness probably entails pain, unconsciousness loss of humanity. I pray I may die well. Meanwhile my body and I, if not identified, are in close tandem. At times I sense a spiritual relation accompanying a reduction in nervous tension – intensity gives way to the peace that passes understanding, and even that relates to the way my body is. Yet I also experience a richness in maturity which will no doubt accelerate in the next ten, twenty or thirty years. I suppose the one thing I am more and more sure of is that somehow 'my life is hid with Christ in God' and so is the life of my pathetic adult son – for whose compassionate death I frequently pray.

THE MUSLIM CONCEPT
OF DEATH

Dr M. A. Zaki Badawi, Principal,
The Muslim College

After memorising the Qur'an and studying in his native Egypt, Zaki Badawi was awarded a scholarship to London University where he gained a first degree in Psychology and a doctorate in Islamic Studies. He went on to teach in Egypt, then at the University of Malaya, both in Singapore and Kuala Lumpur, and afterwards moved to the chair in Islamic Studies at Kano, Nigeria. After a period as Professor of Islamic Studies in Jeddah he was appointed, in 1978, Director of the Islamic Cultural Centre and Chief Imam of the London Central Mosques, posts which he held until 1981. He is now Principal of the Muslim College, London, and Chairman of the Imams' and Mosques' Council and the Islamic Religious Council in London.

'Allah takes the souls at the time of their death and that which has not died in its sleep; He withholds that against which he had decreed death, but loses the other till a stated term.' So proclaims the Qur'an, Sura 39:42. (Death is the absence of the soul from the body permanently. Sleep is also the result of the absence of the soul from the body though only temporarily.)

Death and sleep are very closely connected in the perception of Muslims. A great deal of Islamic literature concerning death is based on dreams. The place of dreams as a source of information can be seen in

Ibu Al-Qayyin's, *Kitab Al-Arwah'* (The Book of Souls). He tells us that during sleep, the soul wanders among the heavenly host and thus acquires a great deal of information about the past and the future. The pure souls return to their bodies without interference from the Devil, hence what they communicate in dreams is the truth. Those that are not pure are intercepted by Satan and thus get confused and the dreams that they experience are false. The early Muslims placed such great confidence in the dreams of the pious that the Kalif, Abu Baker, the first to succeed the Prophet, acted in a case of inheritance, on a dead man's instructions as received in a dream by a companion of the Prophet!

Statements in the Prophetic Tradition warned Muslims to report their dreams truthfully and the Prophet and his followers used to relate their dreams and seek information through their interpretation. Dreams about the dead were accepted as a source, indeed the source of information of life after death.

The Origin of Life

The Holy Qur'an tells us about the beginning of life. 'Behold, the Lord said to the angels: I am about to create a human being from sounding clay, out of dark slime transmuted and when I have formed him fully and breathed into him my spirit, fall down before him in prostration.' (Sura 15:28, 29) It is the spirit of God which turns the inanimate clay into a living being.

The Soul

But what is the nature of this spirit? Where does it reside? With regard to the subject of life and death, we are dependent on the given rather than the acquired information. There are many beliefs about the nature of the spirit of the soul, going back to the ancient civilisations of India, Egypt, Persia and Mesopotamia. There are theories in the subject put forward by Greek philosophers. As a Muslim, however, I depend on the Muslim Scriptures, the Holy Qur'an and the tradition of the Prophet. The Qur'an is silent about the nature of the soul, which silence may even be thought to suggest that the subject is taboo.

In answer to a question by some Jews about the subject, the Qur'an instructed the Prophet to say, 'The soul is a matter for my Lord and you have been granted little knowledge'. (Sura 17:85) Despite this verse, many Muslim scholars theorised on the nature of the soul. They contended that the Qur'anic verse can be interpreted to mean that the soul is created by God or is under his command and therefore there is no barrier to our understanding of its nature as it is not within the exclusive knowledge of God. There are those who thought of it as a divine element which enables the body to move, feel and think as a human being. They support their view by the verse which states that the souls of those who are dead or asleep are with God and he sends back those who are asleep and keeps those of the dead. Some even suggest that souls exist before the creation of man.

They cite the verse 'It was on the occasion when your Lord brought forth from the loins of the children of Adam their offspring and called upon them to bear witness about themselves. "Am I not your Lord?" They answered, "Yes indeed, we bear witness thereto." ' Such gathering of the offspring is indicative that their souls were there before their births. It appears therefore that the souls have an independent existence from the body and may therefore be assumed not to be subject to destruction. Some traditionalists believe the soul to be material, not spiritual, and that it is not in any sense eternal. They cite the Qur'anic verse declaring that everything shall perish except the face of your Lord.

Where Does the Soul Reside?

The consensus of the scholars is that it resides in the whole body. Malik the Jurist of Al-Madinah likens it to the water going through a young plant. It is the invisible element which fits the visible and gives it life.

How Does Death Occur?

Death occurs by the soul departing from the body, beginning with the extremities such as the feet, reaching the thoughts (Sura 39:43) and then leaving the body. The Qur'an's description of the symptoms of the advent of death corresponds to common observation. As the body dies it loses its ability to move voluntarily and becomes flaccid.

Just as the soul was breathed into the body by God, so it departs only through his intervention. According to the Qur'an, there is an angel of death who, singly or with assistants, is in charge of extracting the souls from the bodies of the dying. The tradition names him 'Azrail'. His manner of operation differs. If the dying person is pious, the angel calls his soul to depart to the mercy of God. The soul leaves the body as easily as a 'drop from a waterskin'. It is then wrapped by the angels in a perfumed shroud and lifted to the 'Seventh Heaven' to be recorded and then sent down to rejoin the body for the 'Trial in the Tomb'.

The soul of the unbeliever or the evil-doer is instructed to depart to the 'Wrath of God' and is extracted like a 'skewer through moist wood' – 'the odour from it is like the stench of a decomposed carcass.'

The soul is then taken to the Abyss of Abysses for recording and then returned to be tried in the tomb. The angel of death is visible only to the dying and his image is beautiful and gentle to the pious, but ugly and cruel to the ungodly.

The Trial in the Tomb

The Trial in the Tomb is reported in numerous traditions. It takes place as soon as the tomb is sealed. Two angels, by the names of Munkir and Makir, appear to the entombed and ask him set questions. Who is your God? What is your religion? Who is your prophet? What is your Guide? If the answers are Allah, Islam, Muhammad and the Qur'an, the tomb is broken and filled with all that is pleasurable. If, however, the answers are different in any detail, the angels inflict terrible torture upon the unbelieving dead person, then the tomb closes on the body so that the ribs collapse. No one can escape this examination. Ibu Al-Qayyin reports that a man sought to avoid this encounter with the two angels, but as soon as this was done, God reconstructed his body and asked him, 'Why did you want your body burned and your ashes scattered?' He said: 'Because I feared you so, I wanted to escape the trial of the tomb. God said, 'For being so fearful of me, I forgive you!'

Traditions inform us that animals may hear the sound of the torture in the tomb and even some ordinary people have reported witnessing tombs ablaze with fire and some with light.

Sceptic Muslim scholars reject the tomb trial altogether and regard all reports concerning it as a collection of myths. This, however, is not the view of the vast majority of Muslims, many of whom recite at the tomb the correct answer to the four questions to help the resident of the tomb pass the test successfully. The belief that the dead hear the speech of the living is confirmed by many traditions. Some scholars however, reject this and cite the Qur'anic verse 22 Sura 35, which states, 'You cannot make those in their tombs to hear.' In fact, the Sceptics argued that when bodies are exhumed, they show no trace of ribs being broken or the body altered in any way, other than the normal process of decomposition, which affects the believer and unbeliever alike. The Traditionalists scorn the last argument as applying the laws of this world to a totally different one. The world of the spirit is not constrained by our time-space, nor does it come under our limited observation.

The Burial and Mourning

The deceased is washed and wrapped in white shrouds. A prescribed funeral service (Salat Al-Janazah) is held either in the home or at the grave, but usually at a mosque.

The deceased is placed between the worshippers and the Qiblah, that is, in the direction of the Ka'ba in Mecca. Once the service is concluded the body is taken for burial. It is made to rest on the right side, supported by bricks or stones, facing Mecca. In some Muslim countries cave-like tombs are built to ease the placing of the body in the required position. Once the burial is over and the instructions to the dead are recited, the mourners ask God for mercy on the deceased soul, read the first chapter of the Qur'an (Al-Fatizah) and depart.

The family mourn the dead for three days, except for a wife who has to mourn her husband for four months and ten days. However, if she is pregnant, then her mourning shall end by the birth of her child, provided it does not take place before the mandatory period of four months and ten days. In the view of others, the birth of the child alone signals the end of the period of mourning.

Al-Barzakh

After the Trial in the Tomb, the souls gather in Al-Barzakh which is the time-space separating this world from the Day of Resurrection. Al-Barzakh is, however, not the same for everyone. The pious are housed at the door of Paradise within sight of their intended final homes, which they will occupy after the Day of Judgement. The evil ones, on the other hand, are thrown into the Abyss of Abysses where they suffer torture at the edge of Gehammam (Hellfire).

When the souls of the believers welcome the new-comer, they enquire about their relatives and friends left behind.

The Resurrection

'The trumpet shall be blown and whosoever is in the heavens and whosoever is in the earth shall swoon, save whom God wills.' (Sura 39:68) Then the soul will have gone through four stages. The first when it existed in the world of spirits; the second, when it was breathed into the foetus; the third when, on death, it departed from the body and resided in Al-Barzakh; and the fourth when,

147

on Resurrection, it rejoined the body in eternal unity in
Paradise or Hell.

Modern Issues

The given information about the soul and the nature
of death served Muslims well until the modern developments in medicine and medical technology.

The first issue is the question of autopsy. Muslims
abhor any tampering with the dead body. They regard it
as an aggression against the defenceless and a manifes-
tation of contempt. Even in war, the Muslims were
enjoined by the Prophet not to mutilate the bodies of
their dead enemies as was the prevailing custom in his
day.

Modern physicians need autopsies for research into
various areas of medicine. Criminal investigation also
necessitates autopsy. Many Muslims will go to every
possible length to avoid this happening to any member
of their community.

My second concern is organ transplantation. The vast
majority of scholars support it though, clearly, it involves
interference with a deceased body. They argue, however,
that saving life is a higher principle than the preservation
of the body of the dead.

The question, however, is more complex. The trans-
planted organ has to be extracted while it is still
functioning. A totally dead organ cannot be used for the
operation. A new definition of death will have, therefore,
to be found. The issue is still being debated and the
scholars see no reason to order a halt to the exercises of
transplantation while they resolve it. To be sure, there
are a few voices raised against transplant surgery on the
grounds that it is an illegal use of parts of a human body,

since the family of the deceased do not own his body to give away. Even a living person is not entitled to donate parts of his body because he is not authorised in Muslim law to sell his organs, so he cannot give it as a gift either, for the rule is that 'What you cannot sell, you cannot give as a gift.'

Some of those who permit organ transplant draw the line at the sexual organs. They contend that testicle transplant, for instance, would change heredity, as the offspring will carry the genes of the original owner of the organ, who will therefore be the real father of the children, which makes them illegitimate.

A further problem not yet faced by them is the possibility of brain transplantation. This, I am informed, is theoretically possible. The resultant change of personality will be startling.

My Own Point of View

I begin by declaring my total commitment to Islam. To me, the Qur'an is the received word of God, explained and expounded by the Prophet Muhammad through his words and actions. These are recorded in the literature known as the Tradition of the Prophet. The Scriptures of Islam, that is, the Qur'an and the Tradition (Sunnah), are accepted by me as an act of faith, supported in most cases by reason. No statement in the Scriptures which challenges reason is acceptable. There are, however, areas which are beyond reason rather than against reason and here I would respect the information which comes through revelation.

Bearing this in mind, I accept the statement of the Qur'an that life is breathed by God into every human being. The nature of soul (*ruh* or *nafs* in Arabic) is not defined and the Qur'an gives no statement of its nature. Though the majority of scholars believe it to be spiritual, not material, I am inclined to the view that the soul is no more than a function of matter organised in a particular fashion. It is like the colour that two transparent liquids acquire on being mixed together. Life in the sense of conscious existence depends on the brain.

During sleep, or under sedation or the like, we lose this consciousness, but we are still considered alive. When the brain is irreparably damaged, we die. Through the use of life-support machines we can continue to function in a state of coma for a long time. It appears to me to indicate that 'life' is a function of the operation of bodily organs and not the other way around. Transplant surgery is, therefore, a mechanical operation.

The question, however, that has to be addressed is whether we are entitled to cut up a 'living' body, albeit an irrevocably dying one, to use it as spare parts. There are two principles in contention here. One is the sanctity of the human body, particularly of those who are not competent to speak for themselves. The second is the obligation to save the life of an ailing person. I choose to save one life rather than to lose two for the purpose of transplanting a basic organ such as a heart or a lung. Death will have to be defined in terms of irreversible damage to the function of the brain.

Brain transfer is a theoretical possibility, the consequences of which are staggering. It is likely to cause a total change of personality which is beyond our comprehension at present.

Though the duality between the spiritual and material in man is not taken seriously by me, I am not denying the hereafter. Resurrection does not depend on an eternal element to keep as an anchor to a perishable one. Allah will resurrect our bodies just as he created them and a new life will be breathed into them as it was the first time. I firmly believe in the Resurrection and the Day of Judgement on two grounds. Firstly, the Revelation in the Qur'an and secondly, I believe in God's justice. This world is obviously unjust. The weak and the unwary suffer at the hands of the strong and the devious. I do not believe that the universe is governed by a blind, brutal force. I believe the universe to be the Creation of God, who cannot be unjust. The only way to correct the injustice of this world is through resurrection into another world where human beings would have no freedom to commit transgressions.

The question remains as to how this is to be done and what happens to the bodies that get mixed up together through the process of the food chain or transplant. The answer is that we must be more careful not to apply the physical laws of our world to a world unknown to us. The nature of reward and punishment is a mystery. Our language and our categories of thought are used in the sacred texts in an allegorical way. The hereafter is beyond our comprehension.

All references to life after death I accept as given, not as rationally proven. I, however, do not take dreams to be a source of knowledge concerning the past or a pointer to the future. The earlier scholars who set so much store by dreams did not have as much knowledge of the nature of dreams as we do now.

Whatever the nature of the soul, it is not beyond God to act upon it as he wills. Such issues are beyond our ability to observe or analyse. We can only accept the given knowledge.

ATTITUDES TOWARDS DEATH IN THE TWENTIETH CENTURY

The Rt Revd Richard D. Harries, The Bishop of Oxford

After his early education at Wellington and Sandhurst, and a period as an officer in the Royal Corps of Signals, Richard Harries went first to Selwyn College, Cambridge and then to Cuddesdon College, Oxford before being ordained to work as a curate in Hampstead. He followed this with a period as a college chaplain and then as a member of staff at Wells theological college. Nine years as the vicar of All Saints, Fulham came before his appointment as Dean of King's college, London. In 1987 he was consecrated as Bishop of Oxford. He is well known as a popular broadcaster and writer, with interests that range over a wide variety of topics. He and his wife Josephine are the parents of a son and daughter.

Dr Johnson once walked in the grounds of his old college at Oxford, Pembroke, with a friend. Boswell recorded:

> Dr Johnson surprised him not a little, by acknowledging with a look of horror, that he was much oppressed by the fear of death. The amiable Dr Adams suggested that God was infinitely good. *Johnson,* 'That he is infinitely good as far as the perfection of his nature will allow, I certainly believe; but it is necessary for good upon the

whole, that individuals should be punished. As
to an individual, therefore, he is not infinitely
good; and as I cannot be sure that I have fulfilled
the conditions on which salvation is granted, I am
afraid I may be one of those who shall be damned.'
(looking dismally) *Dr Adams*, 'What do you mean by
damned?' *Johnson* (passionately and loudly), 'Sent
to Hell, Sir, and punished everlastingly.' *Mrs Adams*,
'You seem, Sir, to forget the merits of our Redeemer.'
Johnson, 'Madam, I do not forget the merits of my
Redeemer; but my Redeemer has said that he will
set some on his right hand and some on his left.' –
He was in gloomy agitation, and said, 'I'll have no
more on't.' (*Life of Johnson*, OUP)

If we are to contrast attitudes towards death in
the twentieth century with those of previous ages,
the first point we notice is the fading of any sense of
divine judgement after death. The belief in purgatory,
which arose in the eleventh century and so dominated
the European mind until the Reformation and which is
so vividly expressed in some of the wall paintings of our
churches, no longer terrifies the imagination. It might
be argued that Johnson's fear of divine judgement was
unusually strong because of his fierce sense of inner self
demand or what the Freudians would call 'a strong
super ego'. However, a belief in a God who sentences
people to everlasting punishment remained firmly part
of Christian orthodoxy right through the nineteenth
century. The great Christian social theologian, F. D.
Maurice, was sacked from King's College, London for
denying the everlastingness of hell. In Newman's *The
Dream of Gerontius* which was first published in 1865,
the soul of Gerontius has to face the prospect of demons
who mock him, judgement and purgatory. *The Dream*

of Gerontius was immensely popular even before Elgar
wrote the music, which received its first performance at
the Birmingham Festival on 3 October 1900.

All this, like so much else, was changed with the First
World War for the nation could hardly allow the Church
to consign literally millions of brave young men, who had
died for their country, to yet another torment. They had
suffered enough, they had lost everything without even
the chance to make much of anything, they must have
gone straight to something better – or so the logic of
compassion urges. The twin pressures of bereavement
and patriotism made the mention of hell or even of
an intermediate state rare on the lips of preachers.
Bishop Winnington-Ingram, the then Bishop of London,
reassured the nation:

> Those dear young men they are not dead. They
> were never more alive than five minutes after
> death . . . they love still those they have loved on
> earth, and they live a fuller life than this, a more
> glorious life.

Death was simply the 'gate of life', a phrase often
used. Christ was depicted as the great comrade waiting
the other side to welcome the boys home. This attitude
was not confined to the established Church. Cardinal
Bourne said about the war, 'God has peopled Heaven
with saints who, without it, would hardly have reached
Heaven's door-sill.'

A belief that death opened the way to a fearful
judgement gave way to a belief that death was but
a door into a world that was kinder than the ravaged
violent earth. This later view is well expressed in some
words of Henry Scott Holland, distinguished Canon of
St Paul's and Regius Professor of Divinity at Oxford

from 1910 until his death in 1918. Scott Holland once wrote, in words that are often quoted today at memorial services:

Death is nothing at all. I have only slipped away into the next room. I am I and you are you. Whatever we were to each other that we are still. Call me by my own familiar name. Speak to me in the easy way you always used. Put no difference into your tone. Wear no forced air of solemnity or sorrow. . . Life means all that it ever meant. It is the same as it ever was. There is absolute unbroken continuity. What is this death but a negligible accident? I am but waiting for you for an interval somewhere very near just round the corner. All is well.

The second major shift of emphasis has been away from concentration on the next world to a preoccupation with this one. Two major figures both reflect and help to account for this change, Marx and Freud. Marx was not in fact as hostile to religion as is sometimes supposed. However, he did believe that the human hope which was expressed in religious hope for heaven is a falsification, a misplacing of a hope which should properly be directed towards a transformed earth. As is well known he called religion the opium of the people but the passage in which that expression appears is worth quoting in full, in order to grasp the force of what Marx said. He wrote:

Religious suffering is at the same time an *expression* of real suffering and a protest against real suffering. Religion is the sigh of the oppressed creature, the sentiment of a heartless world, and the soul of soul-less conditions. It is the *opium* of the people. (*Critique of Hegel's Philosophy of Right*)

155

Although there are not many classic Marxists around, his criticism of religious hope has entered deeply into the consciousness of twentieth-century human beings. Very many people, who are far from calling themselves Marxists, see it as the proper and urgent task of human beings to change social and political conditions on earth. Together with this they often regard hope for a life after death as at best a distraction from, or at worst an obstruction to, the prime task.

The same point was made by Freud in rather different terms. He accounted for religion in a number of different ways but one of these was to regard it as the product of wishful thinking, a view that is well summed up in a lapidary statement of Iris Murdoch: 'All that consoles is fake.' Freud, with characteristic eloquence, wrote:

> Of what use to him is the illusion of a kingdom on the moon, whose revenues have never been seen by anyone? As an honest crofter on this earth he will know how to cultivate his plot in a way that will support him. Thus by withdrawing his expectations from the other world and concentrating all his liberated energies on this earthly life, he will probably attain to a state of things in which life will be tolerable for all and no one will be oppressed by culture any more. Then with one of our comrades in unbelief, he will be able to say without regret – let us leave the heavens to the angels and the sparrows.

If we want to obtain the full force of the contrast, we have only to compare the hymns written in the nineteenth century with hymns written in the last decade. The former focus on the joys of heaven and how to attain them, the latter on tasks to be done on this earth and how to achieve them.

These two fundamental shifts of emphasis, the fading of any sense of divine judgement after death and the transfer of interest from the next world to this one, have left a widespread sense of unease and uncertainty about the place of death in human existence. As is well known, for so many death has become a solitary, hidden experience. There are virtually no public mourning rituals now. There remains a wistful hope for some kind of continued existence after death but no lively belief in its certainty or even probability. This may be understandable enough in the population as a whole. However, what is somewhat more surprising is how contemporary Judaism sits light to the prospect of life after death and what a high percentage of Christian church-goers share the current scepticism. Public-opinion polls carried out a few years ago reveal not only widespread disbelief in the possibility of a life after death but also that this disbelief is shared by many regular church-goers. So we have a society in which death is not regarded as a gateway to either hell or heaven. It is simply there, full of foreboding but not properly faced except in some artistic works such as the plays of Samuel Beckett.

At this stage, it might be worth indicating some developments in Christian theology that have taken place in recent decades. First, there has been a demise in talk about the soul. This has come about partly as a result of philosophical scepticism and partly because of a recovery of a more Hebraic way of thinking. Philosophers have been unable to give much sense to the idea of a soul conceived of as a box inside a box inside a box. It is true that there has been a reaction in some quarters, with a call to retain 'soul talk'. It has been urged that soul talk, though not referring to some invisible essence of the human being, is nevertheless essential to refute all forms of reductionism. In order to counter views which see

157

human beings as simply a series of chemical processes or complex cells, talk about the soul reminds us that the human person must be seen as a whole and that the whole is more than the sum of its parts. But this demise, or at least reinterpretation, of language about the soul has gone together with a new emphasis upon the value of Hebraic as opposed to Greek ways of looking at the human being. The Hebrews did not think of human beings as essentially souls imprisoned in bodies. Rather, they thought of human beings as psychosomatic unities. God took the clay of the ground and breathed on it and man became a living being. The Hebrews thought of human beings as a unity of body, mind and spirit. Secondly, and not unconnected with the first point, it has become usual to contrast the way in which Socrates and Jesus approached their respective deaths. Socrates died calmly, looking forward to the release of the eternal soul from its prison in the body. Jesus was 'very sorrowful, even to death' and, according to Luke, with his sweat like great drops of blood falling to the ground, prayed three times in the Garden of Gethsemane that the cup of suffering and death might be removed from him: 'Abba, Father, all things are possible to thee; remove this cup from me.'

Similarly, St Paul viewed death as 'an enemy'. This attitude has surprising resonances in some modern literature.

Reflecting on his father's dying, Dylan Thomas wrote those lines which have since become well known:

> *Do not go gentle into that good night,*
> *Old age should burn and rave at close of day;*

Simone de Beauvoir quoted these words on the first page of her book about the death of her mother, published in 1964, and ironically entitled *Une Mort très Douce (A*

158

Happy Death in the English version). The theme of the book is stated in the final words:

> There is no such thing as a natural death: nothing that happens to man is ever natural because his very presence calls the world in question. Every man is mortal; but for every man his death is an accident and even if he knows of it and consents to it, an untimely violence.

Canon Henry Scott Holland also held death to be an accident, but a 'negligible accident' not *une violence indue*, not an outrage as Simone de Beauvoir held.

Thirdly, and again not unconnected with the previous two points, there has been a recovery of the depth of meaning in the symbol of resurrection. For most of its history the Church has combined the Greek and Hebraic way of looking at what happens after death. It was held that at death the immortal soul was released from the body but that, except in the case of the Blessed Virgin Mary, who was assumed body and soul into heaven, the soul had to wait for its reunification with the body until the general resurrection of the dead at the end of time. Then the actual physical corpuscles of its own body would be revivified and transformed. Few today could go along with this belief, however many paintings of Stanley Spencer are set before us for our edification. But this does not mean that talk about resurrection has no point. It remains a vital Christian symbol, indicating first of all that whatever lies beyond, we will be more truly and richly ourselves than we are now. We will not simply be wispy shades or ghosts. Furthermore, the symbol brings out the point that as this life is sheer gift, so whatever lies beyond is, no less, the gift of God. We go into the darkness of death and it seems the end of all that we are. But God knows us through and through, and that essential being which is each one of us he recreates or reforms in a form and manner appropriate to an eternal existence. We have no right to this, we do not automatically go on in however attenuated form. But we trust that he whose touch we have known now in raising us out of self-preoccupation and despair will touch us again to revivify our essential being for eternity. In some such way those Christian theologians who retain a faith that is recognisably Christian would express the resurrection hope.

It is true that Christian hope for eternal existence has been down-played in many, perhaps most, Christian circles. However, it is not discarded even in those theologians most anxious to emphasise the role of Christianity in transforming this world. The Tübingen theologian Jürgen Moltmann, for example, in his influential *The Theology of Hope*, whose thrust is to nerve us for action in changing the social and economic conditions in which so many still live lives of poverty and oppression, yet maintains that we must have hope, not only for the poor on earth but also hope in the face of death.

Liberation theologians, as the phrase suggests, see the Christian faith as that which liberates us not only from what constricts our personal existence but from all those social, economic and political ills which frustrate that human fulfilment which God has in mind for each one of us. The thrust of liberation theology is to ground and inspire Christian solidarity with and work for the poorest and most oppressed people of the earth. The Vatican, through The Sacred Congregation for the Doctrine of the Faith, has issued two documents on liberation theology. Despite the desire of the press to polarise liberation theologians and the Vatican, the Vatican, whilst making perfectly justifiable criticisms of some forms of liberation theology, is essentially sympathetic to what the liberation theologians are trying to achieve. However, the Vatican documents quite rightly realise that the quest for true justice must include a hope for eternal existence. As *Liberatis Conscientia* puts it:

> For true justice must include everyone; it must bring the answer to the immense load of suffering borne by all the generations. In fact, without the resurrection of the dead and the Lord's judgement, there is no justice in the full sense of the term. The promise of the resurrection is freely made to meet the desire for true justice dwelling in the human heart.

Winston Churchill once said: '. . . there may very well be two worlds, but I prefer to take them one at a time.' The way the modern Christian Church expresses the Christian hope is certainly stronger than that but is not totally unrelated to the priorities that Winston Churchill indicated. It might be put thus. We are to work for the transformation of this world. Under God, our efforts to do so will find their proper fulfilment, if not in this world then in the next.

The attitude C. S. Lewis takes is an interesting contrast with this approach. C. S. Lewis was rather late in coming to a belief in a life after death. When he was a student at Oxford he came to know an old Irish parson, dirty, gabbling and tragic, who had long since lost his faith but retained his living. His only interest in life was the search for evidence of human survival about which he talked non-stop. He did not seek the beatific vision for he did not believe in God. He didn't even seek reunion with his friends. All he wanted was some assurance that something he could call himself would outlive his bodily life. Lewis said that this state of mind appeared to him as the most contemptible that he had ever encountered and the whole question of immortality became disgusting to him. The result was that when Lewis eventually came to believe in God, it was some time after that before he could reconcile himself to a belief in heaven. Yet when he did come to such a belief, it was at the foreground in both his popular writings on theology and his imaginative literature. Towards the end of his life he was accused of placing too much stress upon this aspect of the Christian faith. But, as he said:

> How can it loom less than large if it is believed in at all? If that other world is once admitted, how can it, except by sensual or bustling pre-occupations, be kept in the background of our mind?
> *(Prayer, Letters to Malcolm, Collins, p.120)*

C. S. Lewis is still very influential in some quarters and his books have sold many millions. However, the centrality of the hope for immortality in his thinking has not on the whole been shared by professional theologians. They, as I have tried to show, state the matter somewhat differently. Lewis is instructive by the contrast he makes with professional theologians, who retain a hope for eternal life but who do not isolate it from hope for a better earth.

Given these changes of attitude, the fading of any real sense of divine judgement after death, the shift in emphasis away from the next world to this world, and within theological circles an approach to death which recognises its proper fearfulness and, whilst retaining hope in the face of death, does not make immortality the be-all and end-all of Christianity, what today do we mean by a 'good death'? How can we talk about a 'good death' in a way that remains true to Christian faith and yet which can also engage the sympathy of that wider circle which have no consciously articulated faith?

What then is meant by a 'good death' in our time? First, the management of pain. This is not my sphere, so I do not intend to say anything about it except that I am grateful that through good medical care, the right doses of the right drugs administered at the right times, it is possible to keep patients even in the terminal stages of a distressing illness out of acute pain.

Secondly, a 'good death' is one in which one is able to face up to all those disturbing and unsettling feelings about oneself and others. This, along with so much else, has, as we know, been pioneered by the hospice movement, originating from the work of Dame Cicely Saunders, at St Christopher's. The hospice movement has enabled many patients to deal with the sometimes inevitable guilt, depression and family discord that occur in the crisis of death. Trust is made available, though not pressed, so that the family is enabled to travel together. Within this context patients can search for meaning in a climate of openness and trust. The hospice movement has tried to establish, alongside its commitment to excellence in practice, the affirmation of the individual with all their hopes and fears and a concern for the bereaved family as a whole.

The unsettling feelings which people experience in the approach to death have many facets. But one of them is certainly the sense of loss. In some ways the Bible can be considered as a story of loss, of people being given a land and then losing it, of being given a monarchy and then losing it, and so on. From this point of view Jesus comes as the combination of the sense of loss, both His own sense of loss as his hopes for the Kingdom of God appeared not to be realised and the sense of loss of His disciples after His crucifixion. It is true that the New Testament puts into

163

the mouth of Jesus predictions about His resurrection. However, most New Testament scholars regard these as expressions of the mind of the Church, wise after the event.

A 'good death' is one in which we are enabled to face our negative feelings, in particular our attitude to death itself. There is a long and honourable religious tradition on the theme of preparing for death, on dying before we actually die. The old Prayer Book litany prayed that we may be delivered from 'battle, murder and sudden death'. The theme of leaving time to prepare is never very far away in Graham Greene's novel *Brighton Rock*. Much of this may have had to do with preparing to meet one's Maker suitably contrite and believing. However, the twentieth century can see also in this tradition another wisdom. Doctors know better than anyone the shock of a sudden death. Death, however much expected, is always in some sense a shock. Yet a long illness gives not only the person who is dying but, no less important, family and friends time to adjust and accomplish much emotional business in the period before death finally comes.

A 'bad death' is one in which one dies alone. Of course, there is a sense in which everyone is alone at the end. However, a 'good death' is one in which one has the companionship of other people both in the preparatory period and during the period of passing itself. Here again the hospice movement and hospitals that have been influenced by it have been so helpful in giving, wherever possible, the necessary support and companionship. One of the wonderful features of accounts of the death of saints, of which there are so many in Christian literature, is the description of beloved friends crowding round the bedside weeping, praying, saying farewell and, as often as not, recording a sense of the dying one being welcomed to the other side by a no less loving fellowship. They were

164

communal events. By way of contrast, I was struck, as perhaps you were, by the loneliness of the self-inflicted deaths of Arthur Koestler and his wife. On rational grounds they opted for euthanasia. But it seemed so sad and isolated.

Then, a 'good death' is one which is fully integrated into, and in some sense is, a proper flowering of the person's life. One of the people who seemed to achieve this was, surprisingly, D. H. Lawrence. As he lay dying of TB in 1929, still only in his early forties, Lawrence wrote what must be the most positive poems on death of our century. In 'Shadows' he expresses a biblical faith in one who allows us to sink into oblivion in order to raise us to new life:

> *I am in the hands of the unknown God,*
> *he is breaking me down to his own oblivion*
> *to send me forth on a new morning, a new man.*

Yet it is what is almost the theme music for this sequence that I specially want to note. Another poem begins:

> *Sing the song of death, O sing it!*
> *For without the song of death, the song of life*
> *becomes pointless and silly.*

'Sing the song of death'; this, coming from Lawrence, above all the man of life about whom Frieda wrote, 'Right up to the last he was alive and we both made the best of our days, then he faced the end so splendidly, so like a man.' It is the fact that this song of death comes from Lawrence that is so impressive. Others have welcomed death, none more so than Stevie Smith. Her final lines:

Come, Death, and carry me away . . .
Come, Death. Do not be slow,

express a lifetime's longing for oblivion.

Lawrence's whole life, on the other hand, was protest against that kind of attitude; yet it was he who said: 'without the song of death, the song of life becomes pointless and silly'. In order to sing that song more is required than being able to see death as a way out or through. The gifted preacher and theologian Austin Farrer pointed to that more. In a sermon preached some time during the 1950s when a mission was going on in Oxford University, Austin Farrer considered the problem of our nice worldly friends. Are they to languish for ever in hell? How absurd it seems when we are all laughing together over a pint of beer in a pub.

Man's destiny consists of two parts: first we live and then we die. In the eyes of God our dying is not simply negative, it is an immensely important and salutary thing; by living we become ourselves, by dying we become God's if, that is, we know how to die; if we so die that everything we have become in our living is handed back to the God who gave us life, for him to refashion and use according to his pleasure.

God desires that we should grow, live, expand, enrich our minds and our imaginations, become splendid creatures. He also desires that we should die, should be crucified on the cross of Christ Jesus, should surrender all we have and are to him; and he desires that we should die that death spiritually before we die it physically. Well now, what after all are we to say about our dear, delightful unconverted friends? We must say that so far as their lives are

wholesome or truly human, they are splendid mani-
festations of the power to live; but that they have
not yet learned to die, they have not made even the
first step along that more difficult path which Jesus
Christ opened up for us.

A moving statement, yet those of us who are less sanc-
tified than Austin Farrer still want to ask, 'Why should
I surrender all I am to him? Why should I hand back
to God everything I have become in living?' – questions
that lead us to the heart of faith. First: because surrender
is an acknowledgment of the highest, a discovery via
our hints and guesses of a worthy object of our longing,
the source and standard of all we hold to be true and
good and beautiful. Second: because we come to see
that our very being, all that we are, flows from that
spring. Third: because though we spring up *ex nihilo*
and return to nothing, though we come from the dust
and return to the dust, the mouth which breathed
us into life and sustains us in being utters the world
of promise: not less, but more. Yet we cannot receive
this more except we live in accord with reality, in
particular the reality that we are receivers, dependent
moment by moment for our existence on a source beyond
ourselves. We receive a self and surrender a self, hearing
the promise that we will receive again more than we
handed back.

We live and grow and become a self and our whole
being cries out against the loss of that self. Yet the
Christian faith invites us to make that loss a consciously
willed love of God and man. Few people manage to get the
balance right. The Jesuit theologian and anthropologist,
Teilhard de Chardin, with his passionate affirmation of
all that made for life on the one hand and his creative
acceptance of death on the other, was of the few.

He believed in the divinisation of our activities, in a communion with God through our human strengths. In contrast, however, to the current view of life as a process of physical growth followed by physical decline, Teilhard saw it as a process of growth followed by the possibility of further growth through what he called the divinisation of our passivities. It is a difficult vision to sustain, and when faced by horrible illness or humiliating death in those we know, it must sometimes seem impossible. Everything within us that is healthy, that loves life, rages against the forces that diminish us. Yet Teilhard believed that the forces of diminishment take us to a deeper communion and this was his prayer.

It was a joy to me, O God, in the midst of the struggle, to feel that in developing myself I was increasing that hold that You have upon me . . . Now that I have found the joy of utilising all forms of growth to make You, or to let You, grow in me, grant that I may willingly consent to this last phase of communion in the course of which I shall possess. You by diminishing in You.

. . . grant, when my hour comes, that I may recognise You under the species of each alien or hostile force that seems bent upon destroying or uprooting me. When the signs of age begin to mark my body (and still more when they touch my mind); when the ill that is to diminish me or carry me off strikes from without or is born within me; when the painful moment comes in which I suddenly awaken to the fact that I am ill or growing old; and above all at the last moment when I feel I am losing hold of myself and am absolutely passive within the hands of the great unknown forces that have formed me;

168

in all those dark moments, O God, grant that I may understand that it is You (provided only my faith is strong enough) who are painfully parting the fibres of my being in order to penetrate to the very marrow of my substance and bear me away within Yourself.

(*Le Milieu Divin*)

This brings out the point that, for a Christian, death must in the end be not only an act of self-surrender but a form of trust and an expression of self-offering. Jewish mothers used to teach their children to go to sleep with the words of the psalm on their lips, 'Into thy hands I commend my spirit.' It was, according to Luke, with these words that Jesus himself died, 'Father into thy hands I commit my spirit.' Trust, self-surrender, self-offering, a handing-over of ourselves as totally as possible.

Recently, *The Life of Bishop John Robinson* has been written by Eric James (published by Collins). Two years before he himself died John Robinson preached at the funeral of a girl of sixteen who had died of cancer. In his sermon, John Robinson said that 'God was to be found in the cancer as much as in the sunset.'

As he himself was dying of cancer he told people how that statement had come true for him. It does not mean, he stressed, that God sends cancer to test or try us; such a God would be intolerable. So what did he mean? First, it set him thinking about the cause of cancer. He didn't know the cause but he did know that hidden resentments and unresolved conflicts within us sometimes make their presence felt through physical illness. His cancer made him look at what he called his unfinished agenda and to face, come to terms with, and, stronger than that, embrace things about himself he had tended to hide

away. This is the spirit of God, who searches us
out and knows us, leading us into the truth about
ourselves and a true love of ourselves. Secondly,
he became aware of the many people who cared
for him. No doubt, he said, it was all there before,
but as a result of the cancer he had become aware
through the giving and receiving in his relationships with his family and friends of grace upon
grace. Thirdly, when he was given only a few months
to live he re-examined his priorities and decided to
do only what really mattered. He went on holiday
with his wife; he finished off some scholarly work
and above all he tried to make his life really life;
life with a capital L and not mere existence. This
life, which the New Testament calls 'Eternal Life'
is begun, continued but not ended now. It is not
ended with death but it has to begin and develop
now.

In these three ways John Robinson said he had found God
in his cancer as much as in the sunset. John Robinson's
death was a good death not only for the reasons discussed
earlier but because he discovered meaning and purpose in
the process of dying itself.

Our attitude to the prospect of what might happen
after death is very different in the twentieth century from
all preceding centuries, at least in Europe. Nevertheless,
death is no less with us and the problem and opportunity
of helping people in the different circumstances of our
time to achieve a good death is very much with us.
The Christian faith has still, I believe, many insights
to contribute to this task.

I am a child of the twentieth century and, therefore,
these swirling currents in our understanding of death
have inevitably affected me. I am also, by conscious

choice, an inheritor of the Christian tradition and so I want to be shaped by its central beliefs. I am with all this a particular person with a particular psychology, and so these cultural shifts and religious beliefs will take effect in me in a particular way. So where does that leave me in my personal approach to death?

First, I do not fear death itself. Unlike some people I love the dark. The dark for me does not kindle anxiety or fear but a sense of peace and oblivion, in the positive sense that D. H. Lawrence used the word; oblivion as a passage to fresh life, whether after sleep or the sleep of death. Secondly, however, I do fear the process of dying. The fear of pain is strong. So I cannot but be grateful for living in the twentieth century, with its drugs and sophisticated terminal care. But it is still the process of dying rather than the fact of death itself which scares me.

What of the hereafter? A belief in the hereafter is fundamental to my belief in God. I find it difficult to comprehend how people can believe that there is a loving God whilst treating a belief in the afterlife as a kind of optional extra. For me the Christian faith stands or falls as a whole. The existence of so much human anguish and suffering poses such a large question mark against the existence of a loving God that it is only with the full panoply of Christian faith, including the hope of eternity, that one can live with (not answer) the question. So the traditional four last things, death, judgement, heaven and hell, are as real today as they ever were, though one might interpret them somewhat differently from our forebears in the medieval or Reformation periods.

The God in whom I believe will not sentence me to hell. However, in the light of absolute truth, I will see myself as I am and that will surely be a painful purging process. In his *Four Quartets*, T. S. Eliot writes about the gifts reserved for old age:

171

And last, the rending pain of re-enactment
Of all that you have done, and been; the shame
Of motives late revealed, and the awareness
Of things ill done and done to others' harm
Which once you took for exercise of virtue.
Then fools' approval stings, and honour stains.
From wrong to wrong the exasperated spirit
Proceeds, unless restored by that refining fire
Where you must move in measure, like a dancer.

As we move into the nearer presence of God the re-enactment will be no less painful and the refining fire no less fiercely beautiful.

God will not sentence me to hell because he has shown me in Christ that his love will never let me go. Whatever agonies of self-knowledge I may have to undergo his hand will hold mine and lead me through. About heaven, it is foolish to speculate. All images are inadequate. I am content with the words of the Collect in the Book of Common Prayer:

O God who hast prepared for them that love Thee such good things as pass man's understanding; pour into our hearts such love toward Thee, that we, loving Thee above all things, may obtain thy promises, which exceed all that we can desire; through Jesus Christ our Lord.

How can these things be, when there is nothing in the way of hard evidence? Yet I am troubled less by Hume than by Marx. Pure philosophy in the end leaves metaphysical questions open. Marx, and others, pose a profound moral challenge. How can we talk about the afterlife in a way which does not detract at all from our efforts to improve life in this world? So I am challenged to keep my gaze on this earth, to let God work in and through me to alleviate suffering and enhance human well-being here and now. Nevertheless, there is hope. The Christian faith talks about this hope in terms of Resurrection. I do not believe that my physical body will be resurrected as in some Stanley Spencer painting but the person I truly am will be re-created and re-formed in a manner appropriate to an eternal mode of existence. That is the truth that the doctrine of the Resurrection of the Body safeguards. I will be more richly myself then, with a greater capacity to express myself and communicate with God and others, not simply a wispy shadow. The immortal diamond that is really me will, in the Resurrection, be for ever me.

> *In a flash, at a trumpet crash,*
> *I am all at once what Christ is, since he was what*
> *I am, and*
> *This Jack, joke, poor potsherd, patch, matchwood,*
> *immortal diamond,*
> *Is immortal diamond.*
> Gerard Manley Hopkins, 'That Nature is a Heraclitean
> Fire and of the Comfort of the Resurrection'

Meanwhile, I hope to die as I seek to live, with trust in God, and self-surrender. As I know something of his goodness now I am expecting to know it more fully through the fire of judgement and resurrection.

WHERE DO WE
GO FROM HERE?

The Revd Canon John A. White

To seek to draw some conclusion from this series of approaches to death would be to show a lack of faith in life itself. For, as Frances Young said, 'to live to the full means being open to change' and what we experience through these contributions is the stuff of which change is made. Each writer has inherited a tradition of thought and has shown that such traditions, however loyally served, provide but the language by which we may interpret our individual realisation of the common human experience of life and death. It is that essential commonness of experience, underlying all our diversities of culture and philosophy, which has prompted some people today to pursue what Professor John Hick has called a 'global theology'. Perhaps the less specific contemporary use of the word 'theology' will allow it to include the views of those who hold no religious belief or preserve a conscientious agnosticism. For we need some word by which we may express that reflective openness to life which finds the chief characteristic of the human spirit in the capacity to live creatively with what is necessarily provisional.

There is, of course, nothing provisional about death itself, and knowing this we can sense a pristine freshness about Hermann Bondi's assertion that he finds it difficult to get excited about the alleged philosophical problems of an utterly natural phenomenon. Even Jewish and

174

Christian writers who have, in their common scriptural foundation, a belief that death is the punishment for sin, assuming therefore that humanity was originally created to be immortal, appear to have accepted that human life has a natural terminus. Clearly, speculation is rife when thoughts of the afterlife emerge but it is not only ventures into the metaphysical which make death a subject of reflection and for a 'concentrating of the mind'. This is clear from Hugh Beach's view, made against a Christian background: that preoccupation with immortality can 'corrupt the whole thing' because we need to focus our attention on this life, it 'being all that we are sure of', rather than expend energies 'storing up goodies against a future existence which may never materialise'.

But perhaps the matter of eternal life cannot be dealt with quite so pragmatically. For Richard Harries a belief in the hereafter is fundamental to belief in God. Clearly the idea of 're-birth' is integral to Peter Harvey's Buddhist understanding, 'what I will become will be a development from and beyond what "I" am now'. C. S. Lewis asked: once the idea of posthumous existence was admitted then, save for 'sensual or bustling pre-occupation' could it be kept in the background of our mind? Perhaps during the time since Lewis made that enquiry there has been a growing uncertainty amongst religious people about the possibility of, or need for, an afterlife which might compensate in some way for the miseries of 'the vale of woe', that being the theological proposition Marx astutely criticised for its negative social impact. What does seem apparent amongst all the writers in this collection who wish to hold on to some view of eternal life is the need to expand the vocabulary of images presented by their tradition. Sometimes this expansion is to allow for new ideas and correctives to the ancient othodoxies, sometimes simply to make the

175

essence of those orthodoxies more substantially available for inclusion in our contemporary post-Enlightenment world views.

'Without the song of death, the song of life becomes pointless and silly,' thus D. H. Lawrence understood the place of death in any attempt we may make to understand the nature of our life. Perhaps for some people this may be giving death too great a significance, encouraging it to that 'pride' which John Donne so despised in 'Divine Meditations VI' –

poppie, or charmes can make us sleepe as well,
And better than thy stroake; why swell'st thou then?

For without accepting Donne's belief that 'one short sleepe past' and 'death, thou shalt die', it is possible to take the view that death should be 'kept in its place' and be prevented from dominating our living of this life. The funeral wake, today kept in Britain by some Pentecostal communities, is just such a taming of death. Yet finding 'the proper place' for death may be our greatest human challenge. For our mortality clearly troubles us in a way which the same mortality does not seem to trouble other creatures. Human beings are not simply concerned with survival; we are also concerned with meaning, and death appears to be a great question mark drawn against all our attempts at meaning. Hermann Bondi puts that question mark most acutely for those of a religious spirit: 'As a Humanist I believe in the importance of human linkages, of human interactions, of our lives getting their meaning from our connections with each other.' It is precisely this view, that 'no man is an ilande', which encourages the religious to seek for a reality which is greater than that which can be perceived in the material universe, a

Divine intelligence which calls us to 'love our neighbours as ourself'. This web of love, however, is savagely broken every moment somewhere in the world and those who for a space thought that they had recognised some purpose in life, some meaning in existence, find themselves robbed of half their being and thus left alone and psychologically impoverished, to make some kind of new life from the ruins of the old. Does this give us cause, we may rightly ask, to affirm a benign creative principle, or should we better seek some isolation from others to protect ourselves from hurt and to prepare for the ultimate loneliness of dying?

The English theologian John Hick writes in *Death and Eternal Life* (Macmillan, 1990): 'We shall not be able to refrain from speculating about death until we can refrain from speculating about life; for the one is inseparable from the other.' We grow daily more aware, in our dangerous world, of the need for greater human co-operation and an increased sense of communality. For some this will only emerge when we have become a truly secular society. Others take more seriously the legacy of language, belief and thought, which is part of our human inheritance, and seek to look for ways of using that in approaching some kind of 'global theology' which does not seek to destroy traditions but to capitalise upon them. Jonathan Magonet is correct when he writes, 'We lack even a common language of faith with which to begin a conversation with each other.' Yet perhaps our way to finding such a language, transcending diversity of religion and philosophy, will open up as we look more closely at how we all use our traditional and cultural backgrounds in seeking to express our deeper personal awareness and responses to life and to death. For in appreciating the limitations and opportunities offered by all cultures and religions in the pursuit of truth we may discover that we are already closer than we suppose in our common human pilgrimage. In coming face to face with the realities of life and death, survival and extinction, the discovery of meaning and purpose, we need to share our insights and strengthen our common determination to live positively in the creative framework of change.